BATTLES OF THE
ENGLISH CIVIL WAR

Austin Woolrych was educated at Westminster School, commanded a troop of tanks at the battle of El Alamein and went belatedly to Pembroke College, Oxford. He taught at the University of Leeds until 1964 when he became the first Professor of History in the University of Lancaster and, between 1971 and 1975, Pro-Vice-Chancellor. Since retiring in 1985 he has been elected a Fellow of the British Academy and received an honorary D.Litt from Lancaster University.

Also by Austin Woolrych

Commonwealth to Protectorate (Phoenix Press)

Oliver Cromwell

Penruddock's Rising, 1655

Soldiers, Writers and Statesmen of the English Revolution

England Without a King 1649–1660

Complete Prose Works of John Milton (Ed.)

BATTLES OF THE
ENGLISH CIVIL WAR

Austin Woolrych

PHOENIX
PRESS

5 UPPER SAINT MARTIN'S LANE
LONDON
WC2H 9EA

A PHOENIX PRESS PAPERBACK

First published in Great Britain
by B.T. Batsford Ltd in 1961
This paperback edition published in 2000
by Phoenix Press,
a division of The Orion Publishing Group Ltd,
Orion House, 5 Upper St Martin's Lane,
London WC2H 9EA

A CIP catalogue record for this book
is available from the British Library.

Printed and bound in Great Britain by
Butler & Tanner Ltd, Frome and London

ISBN 1 84212 175 8

CONTENTS

ACKNOWLEDGEMENTS

The portrait of Charles I is reproduced by gracious permission of Her Majesty The Queen.

The Author and Publishers also wish to thank the following for permission to include the illustrations which appear in this book:

The Ashmolean Museum

The Trustees of the British Museum

The Trustees of the Chequers Trust

The Church Missionary Society

The Trustees of the Goodwood Collection

The Dowager Lady Hastings

C. H. Lewis, Esq., MBE, Headmaster, Kimbolton School, Huntingdon

Landesgalerie Hanover

The National Portrait Gallery

The Earl of Spencer

WHY JUST THREE battles, the reader may well ask. The answer is that this book first appeared in a series that had hitherto devoted each volume to a single action, whether military or naval. When invited to contribute, I felt I could hardly write about any one Civil War battle at the same length as the publishers had thought appropriate to (say) Waterloo or Mons; Marston Moor was the only one in which either side mustered as many as 20,000 men, and the paucity of professional training and previous military experience in the England of the 1640s meant that tactics had to be kept relatively simple. Whole books *have* been written on single Civil War battles, but they are addressed to fellow-enthusiasts with a specialist's interest in the subject, and so they rightly enter into much fine detail. Writing as I was for the general reader, it seemed to me that if I focused on three major battles I could sufficiently tell the story of each without inflating it, and at the same time convey the nature of the armies, the character of the fighting, and something of what it felt like to be marching or riding into action for king or parliament three and a half centuries ago. And since most of the officers and many of the men on both sides were fighting for causes that they passionately believed in, rather than just for pay or plunder, I had to give proportionally more space than military historians commonly do to the political and religious issues, both as they first led to open war in 1642 and as they underwent modification in the course of the fighting.

It was not hard to select three battles that stand out for their historical importance and their intrinsic military interest. Marston Moor was not only the biggest; it was the first great parliamentary victory, and northern England was thenceforth lost to the king. Naseby blooded the New Model Army and decided the outcome of the first Civil War. Preston even more decisively settled the outcome of the second, and set Charles I on the road to the scaffold. Only Dunbar and Worcester had results of possibly comparable significance, but they belonged to the Commonwealth's later war with Scotland rather than to the English Civil Wars as generally understood.

On re-reading this, my first book, I am very conscious of how much work has been done on its period in the forty years and more since I wrote it. The possibility of revising it was ruled out by various personal commitments to which I felt I had to give priority; and perhaps extensive rewriting would have impaired whatever freshness and integrity it may possess as it stands. If I *had* attempted a revision, I don't think I would have wanted to change much in the chapters on the battles themselves. The urge to tinker would have been stronger in my sketches of the background to the war and of the issues that precipitated and sustained it, for these are the areas where research and revision have been busiest. I now recognise, for example, that the tension between the Court and the Country was a more complex affair than the over-simple confrontation suggested in chapter 1, and I would have been more respectful of the culture of Charles I's court. I now accept that matters of religion determined the allegiance of many more people than I used to think, even though the breaking-points in 1642 were primarily political. I would like to have given more weight to the peerage and the House of Lords in the process of political decision-making. But at least I steered clear of the various brands of determinism, Marxist and other, that still bedevilled the study of the English Revolution around 1960. One thing is sure: revision would have made the book longer, for the almost inevitable effect of close historical research and reappraisal is to make our picture of the past more complicated.

Short of revision, it may be helpful to name some of the many books that have enriched our knowledge of the Civil Wars since this one was written. As a general survey of this whole context, Derek Hirst, *England in Conflict, 1603–1660:*

Kingdom, Community and Commonwealth (1999) is outstanding, and so for its short time-span is G. E. Aylmer, *Rebellion or Revolution? England 1640–1660* (1986). Rather more focused on the wars than those other broad-based accounts: Robert Ashton, *The English Civil War: Conservation and Revolution, 1603–1649* (1978), John Kenyon, *The Civil Wars of England* (1988) and Martyn Bennett, *The Civil Wars in Britain and Ireland, 1638–1651* (1997). Controversy still attends the causes of the wars; compare Ann Hughes, *The Causes of the English Civil War* (Second Edition, 1998), Conrad Russell, *The Causes of the English Civil War* (1990), the same author's *The Fall of the British Monarchies, 1637–1642* (1991) and Anthony Fletcher, *The Outbreak of the English Civil War* (1981). Books concentrating on military history include P. Young and R. Holmes, *The English Civil War* and the collection edited by John Kenyon and Jane Ohlmeyer, *The Civil Wars: A Military History of England, Scotland and Ireland, 1638–1660* (1998). Ian Gentles has written a full and excellent account of *The New Model Army in England, Ireland, and Scotland, 1645–1653* (1992), and I have probed the army's role in politics between Naseby and Preston in *Soldiers and Statesmen* (1987). On the events that led from Preston to the execution of the king see David Underdown's masterly *Pride's Purge* (1971). On the king's forces we have Ronald Hutton, *The Royalist War Effort, 1642–1646* (1982) and two books by Peter Newman, *Royalist Officers in England and Wales, 1640–1660: A Biographical Dictionary* (1981) and *The Old Service: Royalist Regiment Colonels and the Civil War, 1642–1646* (1993). Two valuable topographical guides to the campaigns are Peter Gaunt, *The Cromwellian Gazetteer* (1987) and Peter Newman, *Atlas of the English Civil Wars* (1985).

On the particular battles described in the book the most important recent contributions are Peter Newman, *The Battle of Marston Moor* (1981) and Glenn Foard, *Naseby: The Decisive Campaign* (1995). Both offer very full narratives, and Foard's is particularly valuable for its skilful use of archaeological evidence. Peter Young's *Marston Moor* (1970) and *Naseby* (1985) are disappointingly slight on the actual battles, but Barry

Denton, who has also published several brief regimental histories, offers an attractive concise account in *Naseby Flight*
(1988). The sad news for battlefield-lovers is that despite fifteen
years of persistent effort by the Society for the Preservation of
the Battlefield of Naseby a motorway link has been driven
through an integral part of its site. Little new has been published
on the battle of Preston.

On the actual experience of soldiering in the 1640s Charles
Carlton has written vividly and perceptively in *Going to the
Wars* (1992), and several books have explored the impact of the
Civil Wars on the country at large. They include two fine
collections edited by John Morrill, *Reactions to the English Civil
War* (1982) and *The Impact of the English Civil War* (1991), and
Martyn Bennett, *The Civil Wars Experienced: Britain and Ireland,
1638–1661* (2000). On the interaction between local and national
politics, and the experience of the localities generally, John
Morrill's *Revolt in the Provinces: The People of England and the
Tragedies of War* (1999) is even finer than its earlier version *The
Revolt of the Provinces*, and contains much new matter.

On the biographical front the Cromwell industry continues
to flourish. Two admirable brief lives are Peter Gaunt's *Oliver
Cromwell* (1996) and Barry Coward's *Oliver Cromwell* (1991),
while Christopher Hill's *God's Englishman* (1970) is a brilliant
if not uncontroversial thematic study. John Morrill marshals an
impressive range of contributors to his collection *Oliver
Cromwell and the English Revolution* (1990), and for the Cromwell
Association Peter Gaunt has gathered a score of shorter pieces
in *Cromwell 400* (1999). Antonia Fraser's *Cromwell, Our Chief of
Men* (1973) is a sound biography which will not disappoint her
admirers. John Wilcox, *Fairfax* (1985) and Maurice Ashley,
Rupert of the Rhine (1976) are both good popular biographies,
but Frank Kitson, *Prince Rupert: Portrait of a Soldier* excels on
his military operations. On the king we now have Michael B.
Young's useful *Charles I* (1997), while among straightforward
biographies Charles Carlton, *Charles I* (1983) is the best in a
surprisingly disappointing field.

Since the last edition of this book, one of the friends whose help I gratefully acknowledge in it, Dame Veronica Wedgwood, has died. For the artistry of its narrative, its humanity and its insight into character, *The King's War, 1641–1647* (1958) remains unsurpassed.

Burton-in-Kendal, Carnforth   AUSTIN WOOLRYCH

The Battles of the Civil War

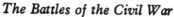

PROLOGUE

TURNHAM GREEN

ALARM AND EXHILARATION were strangely mingled
in the City of London during the early days of November 1642.
The incredible had come to pass: the King was marching on
his capital at the head of a confident army. When he had raised
his standard at Nottingham in August the question had been
whether he would find enough men to fight at all. Not only had
he done so, but the first real battle, at Edgehill on 23 October,
had been much more to his advantage than his enemies'. A
thoroughly confused affair it had been, with both sides claiming
the victory which neither had really won. The troops of both
armies were so raw, and most of their officers so ignorant of
their business, that their reaction to fire and cold steel had
been as various as it was unpredictable. But a battle is judged
by its results, and after Edgehill the Parliament's forces under
the Earl of Essex retired to Warwick to lick their wounds,
leaving the way to London wide open. Fortunately for Parliament and City, Charles was slow to seize his opportunity. The
Earl of Forth, his nominal General-in-Chief, and Prince
Rupert, his most brilliant soldier, urged him to strike at London before the rebels could recover. But Charles could not easily
bring himself to so drastic an act of war while the last chances
of a negotiated settlement remained open. He paused to secure
the surrender of Banbury, then made a triumphal entry into
Oxford, which was to be his headquarters for the rest of the
war. It was another six days before he advanced as far as Reading, on 4 November.

By that time Essex was at Woburn, falling back on London
by a more northerly route across the Chilterns. Despite the
King's slow pace it was doubtful whether he would be able to
throw himself between the royal army and its greatest prize.
Robert Devereux, Earl of Essex, was a mediocre general even

by the amateurish standards of the Civil War, and his military experience on the continent had been slight and unimpressive. But it was more than most peers on the Parliament's side could boast, and for the respectability of the cause and the support of the waverers in the Upper House it was thought essential to have a great nobleman in command. He had none of the allure that had endeared his father to the ageing Elizabeth, nor that hotness of the blood that had carried him into reckless rebellion. The Lord General was stout, serious and slow. But John Pym, the two Houses and the City all knew they could trust him, and in those days, when so many were trimming their sails to every change of the wind, his perfect faithfulness and his doggedness in adversity were qualities not to be lightly prized. He had gone off on campaign with his coffin, his winding-sheet and an escutcheon to grace his funeral – more of a profession of faith in his cause than might be thought, for had it been defeated he might well have followed his father to a traitor's death. And defeat was no distant prospect as the King marched towards London.

Even as he marched, however, efforts were resumed to find some eleventh-hour agreement which would avert the full horror of civil war. Hitherto they had come mainly from Charles's side; now the new turn of fortune drew them from Westminster. On 3 November Parliament asked him to receive commissioners with proposals for a treaty, and he agreed on condition that it sent none whom he had named as traitors. Two peers and four MPs were promptly chosen. But when their safe-conduct to the King's headquarters arrived on the 7th, Parliament was indignant to find one of its nominees, Sir John Evelyn, struck off; Charles had proclaimed him a traitor just a few days ago. Both Houses took this for a mere pretext to postpone negotiation till he saw what force would achieve, and voted that it amounted to a refusal to treat.

Meanwhile the City was preparing with growing urgency to defend itself. Gunners stood by their cannon at every gate and in each main street, their match lit for instant action. Both men and women were busy digging entrenchments and throwing up defence works at the various approaches – St James's, Hyde Park Corner, Piccadilly, St Giles in the Fields, Pancras Fields, Gray's Inn Lane, Holloway Road, Hoxton – while leading men of both Houses rode round these outposts to encourage the work and hearten the soldiers manning them. For the protection of the Houses themselves at Westminster, armed ships were brought up from the docks through London Bridge. The City's militia, the trained bands, were of course embodied, and as many as possible of the Surrey, Hertfordshire and Essex trained bands were brought into such covering positions as Kingston, Watford and Brentford. It was a relief when Essex rode in with the tired remnants of his army on the 7th, but they were far too few to face the royal army alone. Thousands of his soldiers had deserted at Edgehill or after, and though he invited them to return on the tactful assumption that they had 'gone to visit their friends', and got Parliament to offer a bonus to all who were back with their colours in time, many more men were needed. The Puritan preachers spurred their people to their duty, Parliament indemnified all apprentices against being penalized by their masters for enlisting, while the City fathers fixed maximum prices for the soldier's victuals (his beer was not to cost him more than three halfpence a quart). On the 8th Lord Brooke and Sir Henry Vane went to the Guildhall to press the City to fresh efforts. The royalist infantry, Brooke announced, was now about Staines; Rupert had been repulsed at Windsor Castle, but his cavalry was already close to Kingston. Tomorrow, in a final effort, London must raise all the men she could. 'When you hear the drums beat', urged Brooke, 'say not "I am not of the trained band", nor this, nor that, but doubt not to go out to work and fight courageously, and this shall be the day of your deliverance.' Next day the drums brought 9000 apprentices and others to the new artillery ground near Finsbury Field, where Essex and an impressive group of peers and MPs took their pick of them.

But Parliament now had second thoughts about closing the door on negotiation. Evelyn begged the Commons not to let the peace of the kingdom hang on a point of honour concerning himself, and the upshot was that the other five commissioners waited on the King on the evening of the 10th, to request him to name a place near London where he would be prepared to treat. Charles was then at Colnbrook; he had advanced from Maidenhead that morning. He sent the commissioners back next afternoon with a gracious message, suggesting Windsor if Parliament would withdraw its garrison, but undertaking to receive its proposals wherever he might be. His answer seemed to imply a truce, so Essex's army, which had been ordered out on the 10th to its posts on the approaches to London, was now commanded to refrain from hostile actions. But to make sure a messenger was to be sent to the King next day, Saturday the 12th, to request a formal concession of arms.

That messenger never got through. Whether Charles's thoughts ran most on a successful treaty with a frightened Parliament or on a sudden conquest of London we cannot know, but it was typical of him to countenance two quite incompatible lines of action simultaneously. Rupert at any rate thought only of military advantage, and the next move was Rupert's. Early that Saturday morning he set out with a picked body of horse and foot against Essex's outpost at Brentford, ten miles along the road from Colnbrook to London. A thick mist covered his movements, and the news that the King was ready to treat had relaxed the vigilance of Denzil Holles's red-coats, the only regiment (an infantry one) in Brentford itself. They did not know of Rupert's approach until he was a bare mile away. Some musketeers posted in Sir Richard Wynn's house on the river Brent held him up briefly at the entrance to the town. Beyond that he found barricades across the streets, covered by concealed cannon, and he had to call up some of his Welsh infantry. But though Holles's men kept up a fight for over three hours, they were driven back through the town at push of pike on to the open ground towards Turnham Green. Just when their powder and shot were exhausted, Lord Brooke's regiment and then John Hampden's came at last to their support, but not before many of them had been either captured or drowned in trying to escape across the Thames. Towards nightfall the action was broken off and Rupert drew his men back into Brentford. They plundered the town ruthlessly and indiscriminately; the young German Prince had been trained in a school of war which taught little respect for civilian property. But when his uncle the King came up with the rest of the army, Rupert had a dozen guns and colours and several hundred prisoners to show him for the day's work.

Essex was sitting in the Lords when news of the attack reached London early in the afternoon, and it was too late to save Brentford that day. But the whole City, indignant at what it regarded as the King's breach of faith, was quickly roused to a tremendous effort to save its threatened liberties and its still more threatened riches. Every available company, whether of Essex's army or the trained bands or the new levies, was ordered to a general rendezvous at Turnham Green, and all that Saturday night London poured forth a stream of soldiers along the western road. On Sunday morning, when the royal army drew out in battle order on the eastern edge of Brentford, it found itself confronted by 24,000 men, well placed for defence amidst a criss-cross of hedges and ditches. The untried regiments of citizens were posted between those of Essex's which had seen some action, and their commander Major-General Skippon, a brave old Puritan soldier who had risen from the ranks in the Dutch service, moved from company to company exhorting them in homely terms. 'Come, my boys, my brave boys', he cried, 'let us pray heartily and fight heartily; I will run the same fortunes and hazards with you. Remember the cause is for God, and for the defence of your selves, your wives and children.' Many peers and members had come from Westminster to the field in arms, and some of them accompanied Essex as he rode round the regiments encouraging them, while the soldiers threw up their caps and cried, 'Hey for old Robin!'

For most of Sunday the two armies faced each other at about half a mile's distance, both drawn up as for battle with their infantry in the centre and cavalry on either flank. Even now

Charles seemed to assume that he could fight or treat at will. A courtier named White, escorted by a trumpeter, rode forward with a message to the Parliament, declaring speciously that the King had been forced to attack by the advance of Essex's army (which in fact had not advanced since the exchange of messages on Friday), and inviting the Houses to send him their propositions at Brentford. White was blindfolded on reaching the parliamentarian lines and brought before Essex. Just as Essex was reading his letter, the sound of musketry and gunfire broke forth from the Brentford direction. Essex, angrily suspecting treachery, had White and his trumpeter clapped into prison. But the firing came from Syon House, which the royalists had occupied the day before, and was directed against a couple of barges which were carrying men and munitions to the parliamentary garrison at Windsor. After a brisk exchange the men had to be landed and one of the barges blown up, to save its cargo from capture.

In the end there was no battle on Turnham Green. Essex's cannon fired a few rounds, but did little execution. For the royalists, tired, hungry and outnumbered by more than two to one, to attack would have been madness. This was no ground for Rupert's cavalry, with musketeers lining the hedges of the dense enclosures and well-emplaced guns covering every road and passage. On the parliamentary side, the politicians and amateurs were for taking the offensive, the professional soldiers dead against it. Essex meditated a flank attack on the King's left, and actually sent off six regiments towards Acton, but on second thoughts he recalled them. He was wise. There was no knowing how much the martial ardour of his Sunday soldiers would stand up to, and by merely blocking the King's advance he had gained one of the vital decisions of the Civil War. A mood between holiday and heroics marked the whole occasion; it would be well not to test it too far. On the field there were two or three hundred Londoners who had ridden out purely as spectators; the slightest hostile move by either army sent them galloping towards home, and every time they did so a few faint-hearted citizen-soldiers slipped away from their colours.

Meanwhile in London the preachers were urging their flocks from their Sunday morning pulpits to remember their gallant defenders, and at least not to let them go hungry. By midday thousands of goodwives and sweethearts were carrying all they could spare from their larders, and often the best part of their own Sunday dinners, to be loaded at the Guildhall. Nearly a hundred carts rolled out that afternoon to Turnham Green, laden with joints and pies and provisions of all kinds, with quantities of beer and even hogsheads of sack and burnt claret to wash them down. By the time they arrived the troops were ready for them. The King's army was falling back through Brentford, its retreat covered by its dragoons. The beer was specially welcome, for there was none left in Brentford when the parliamentarians marched in; the plunderers had drunk all they could and then knocked in the ends of the barrels, leaving the ale-house cellars awash.

The City's alarms were not quite over. The royalists occupied Kingston, whose garrison Essex had withdrawn to swell the forces on Turnham Green and whose bridge was the first to cross the Thames west of London. Essex had cut the bridge, but the local inhabitants, who were mostly for the King, had laid planks across the gap for his forces to cross. There were fears that Charles would carry them into Kent, where he had many influential sympathizers, and Essex hastily had a bridge of boats built at Putney. But the threat did not develop. Charles rested at Hampton Court for a day, then after a brief stay at Oatlands pulled back his forces to Reading. By the end of the month he was back at Oxford, and London could breathe again.

1

Background to Civil War

THUS A CITIZEN army determined, as another was to do
at Valmy just a century and a half later, that a revolution
would not succumb to force of arms. But it had been a close
enough thing to shock the men at Westminster, who had confi-
dently expected a single short campaign to bring the King to
terms. The first round had shown them that if there were to be
any sudden victory it would be the King's. It forced them to
consider again what they were fighting for, and whether it was
worth a protracted civil war. We too may pause to see what
had brought the two sides to blows, for this was not at all
the sort of war in which the fighting men could leave the
politics to the professionals. Politics were of its essence; politicians commanded regiments and armies, and soldiers could
hardly avoid becoming politicians. It was a war of causes rather
than of survival, and to enter in any way into the minds of
the men whom we shall meet on its battlefields, we must know
what those issues were for which they were ready to risk their
lives and inheritances.

The past forty years had pierced with sharp discords that
subtle harmony between government and society, 'court' and
'country', which the Tudors had contrived. It was not the
Stuarts' fault that they inherited a crown impoverished by rising
prices in a country which was fast growing richer, and a Parliament which had become the mouthpiece of a powerful and
highly articulate governing class. But it was much more their
fault that they antagonized this class until by 1640 all but a
small court clique within it was bent on curbing the crown's
arbitrary powers. The richer gentry who dominated the House
of Commons, and the influential minorities of rich merchants
and lawyers who sat with them and shared their interests, were
often ill-informed and irresponsible in their opposition during

these forty years, and seldom quite disinterested. But the core of their complaint was a passionate protest against incompetence, extravagance and corruption, and against England's steep decline to insignificance in the counsels of Europe. Protestantism and nationalism had been the twin fires which forged national unity under Elizabeth, and Stuart policy seemed a negation of both.

James I's weakness for gaudy young men and worthless sycophants had caused the quality of government to slump sharply; 'he did not chose men for his jobs, but bestowed jobs on his men'.[1] George Villiers, Duke of Buckingham, the most flamboyant of the royal favourites, held an even greater sway over Charles I than over James, until he fell to an assassin's knife in 1628. The Tudor court had offered a career open to the talents, and competition for the glittering rewards of the royal service had helped to keep nobles and gentry in loyalty and discipline. But now the hand that distributed those rewards had grown capricious, and the terms of service less honourable. Entry into the race was becoming hideously expensive, too, with more and more offices being bought and sold at higher and higher prices. This traffic did not profit the King so much as the holders themselves, who regarded their offices as pieces of property from which they could be ejected only for the grossest misconduct. For a decade, Buckingham so ruled the King's servants that the highest or the meanest appointment could depend on his smile or frown, and his favours were expensive. Moreover in the futile wars of the sixteen-twenties, Buckingham's incompetence and the general rottenness in the administration led to a series of disasters to English arms which moved the whole nation to anguish and fury. The memory of Elizabeth's reign, kept alive by the annual bonfires and junketings on her Accession Day, was becoming one of the Stuarts' biggest liabilities. No wonder that Parliament after Parliament split along the lines of 'court' and 'country', with the independent gentry of the latter group combining against the whole gang of courtiers and office-holders, and against Buckingham above

1. H. R. Trevor-Roper, in *History Today*, Vol. V, p. 573.

all. Nor did Buckingham's death remove the trouble, for the next year's session rose to such a pitch of opposition that when Charles dissolved this Parliament he resolved never, if he could help it, to call another.

By this time a new quarrel over religion had added fuel to the many old ones over finance and the royal prerogative. Puritanism was not new, of course, but for a generation past it had been more or less safely contained within the bounds of the Church of England. Little sects like that which sent the Pilgrims over the Atlantic were the exceptions which proved the rule. But when Charles began bestowing the highest places in church and state upon a new school of Anglican divines, dubbed Arminians and led by William Laud, it was not only the Puritans who objected. And the Arminians were not only detested for the altars and vestments and ceremonial which they reintroduced into Anglican worship, or for their anti-Calvinist theology, though to men brought up in the Elizabethan tradition all these things smacked of popery. They also used the pulpit to proclaim that every royal command must be obeyed unquestioningly as a religious duty. They took the old and well-accepted belief in the divine right of kings and inflated it into a novel doctrine of royal absolutism. The bishops claimed divine right for their own order, too, and their sacerdotal pomp and pretensions were the harder to bear because many of them were quite humbly born. Anti-clericalism never lay far beneath the surface among the gentry of England. It rose the higher now because Laud was striving to restore to the church some of the material wealth of which it had been plundered since the Reformation, a work which hardly endeared him to landowners who battened on impropriated tithes or leased fat episcopal manors at easy rents.

No Parliament met for eleven years after 1629, and Charles set out to reconcile his people to a royal government that would rule firmly and benevolently, above the clamour of faction. Over most of Europe the tide was set in favour of personal monarchy and against such representative institutions as Parliament. But England would not have it. Once, she had welcomed

Tudor autocracy as her saviour from anarchy, and good government had meant strong government; but the Tudor peace had done its work too well. It had also rested, necessarily, on the willing co-operation of lords lieutenant, sheriffs, justices of the peace, town corporations and many other local unpaid officials, and these men, in a sense the real rulers of England, had an almost mystical faith in Parliament and the common law. Charles's personal rule fell much too far short of its good intentions ever to come near converting them.

Charles had two men of real stature in his service. Viscount Wentworth and Archbishop Laud both sought to inject the gangrened organism of the state with the old Tudor energy, discipline and paternalism, and a strange friendship grew up between the sombre and vehement man of action, scion of a proud Yorkshire house, and the irascible little red-faced cleric whose father had been a draper in Reading. But neither Wentworth's vision of a noble harmony between the head and members of the body politic, nor the vigour with which he attacked oppression and corruption, impressed contemporaries so much as the ruthless disregard of the letter of the law with which he hounded his opponents or the vast personal fortune he was carving out of the public service. The times no longer condoned the suppression of tyranny by tyranny. As for Laud, his concern for the poor, the unemployed and the exploited was expressed in ways which exasperated the powerful without winning the support of the inarticulate masses. His very presence in the Privy Council, together with two other prelates, was bad enough in anti-clerical eyes; worse still was his use of the Court of Star Chamber to inflict savage punishment on the critics of his order.

Not that these years of personal rule were really dominated by either Wentworth or Laud. Wentworth, whom Charles was slow to trust, was kept far from court, first in York and then in Dublin, while Laud was too much out of tune with his fellow-councillors and courtiers. The King's counsels were ruled far more by what these two men called 'the Lady Mora', signifying delay or hindrance – the spirit of obstruction and procrastination which shelved uncomfortable problems and lived from hand to mouth. It dwelt among the intriguers, the nest-featherers and the ornamental nonentities who made up the common run of the King's servants; it inhabited the throne itself. Laud himself sadly described Charles as 'a mild and gracious prince who knew not how to be, or be made, great'. No Stuart ever conceived the responsibilities of kingship more highly than Charles I. Yet this melancholy, thin-blooded, fastidious monarch lacked the essential zest for the exercise of power and the sheer application of business without which autocracy must fail. 'The duties imposed on him by God he fulfilled with a kind of petulant distaste that struck a chill into those around him.'[1] But he fulfilled them laxly and intermittently. Finer in the grain than either his father or his eldest son, he had the native indolence of both without either the intelligence or the shrewd sense of realities which pulled them up on the brink of deep trouble.

The court was, or should have been, the stage on which the King presented himself to his people, a semi-public spectacle which made Majesty visible and accessible. But since Charles wholly lacked the Tudor flair for courting his people, his court became remote from them, the province of a clique, in whose ears their aspirations and grievances were but a distant murmur. The rift between court and country deepened through mutual ignorance as well as mutual distrust. Charles's court was not vicious and disorderly as his father's had been; indeed in its decorous formality and its leadership of taste and fashion there has been nothing like it since. Charles was the last connoisseur King of England, and in the arts at least he was wonderfully served. But the brittle exquisiteness of the court ideal struck no chord in the philistine heart of England, and the flatteries of the court poets merely encouraged him in his fatal *penchant* for taking his intentions for deeds. Sumptuous and tedious masques, celebrating quite imaginary triumphs of statecraft, hung a curtain of trite allegory and tinsel platitude before the harsh realities of the realm without.

1. J. P. Kenyon, *The Stuarts*, p. 84.

To those outside this stiff world of fantasy and convention it seemed rotten at the core. The Queen was a papist, surrounded by papists; three of the King's chief ministers were of the same persuasion, and it was easy (though unjust) to suspect the Arminian divines and even the King himself of leaning the same way. The crowds in the Queen's chapel, the fashionable conversions, the succession of papal agents at court, the free movement of priests and Jesuits, the virtual suspension of the anti-Catholic laws, all seemed to betoken a monstrous popish plot. Worst of all was Charles's foreign policy. The beloved Princess Elizabeth, Charles's sister and mother to Prince Rupert, shared a helpless exile with her husband, the Elector Palatine, while their principality lay occupied by Spanish troops. Yet Charles reverted all through the thirties to his father's old *rapprochement* with Spain. Each year the Spanish forces which fought the Protestant Dutch in the Low Countries were paid from bullion which had been landed at Plymouth to evade interception in the Channel, minted in England and shipped at Dover in English vessels. In 1639 similar rights of transit were extended to Spanish troops, to the outrage of both national and religious sentiment.

The court which hatched these policies was not only unpopular, it was extremely expensive. Laden with sinecures, wasteful and inefficient, a labyrinth whose ramifications constantly extended themselves of their own parasitic momentum, the royal household defied a whole series of attempts at reform. In the early thirties it was costing more than forty per cent of the King's total revenue.[1] And since there was now no Parliament to meet the King's needs with subsidies, this revenue had to be found by other means. Wherever the letter of the law could be stretched to the King's financial advantage, the crown lawyers stretched it. Obsolete laws were revived for the sole purpose of subjecting 'offenders' to swingeing fines, while the exactions of the hated Court of Wards rose steeply. Merchants and manufacturers found their interests tampered

1. G. E. Aylmer, 'Attempts at administrative reform, 1625–40', *English Historical Review*, LXXII, p. 246.

with in a dozen mischievous ways which bled producer and consumer alike. Ship money seemed at first more reputable, until it was extended to the inland counties and levied annually; then it was resisted as a blatant evasion of the principle of parliamentary consent to taxation.

Just how long Charles's personal rule might have continued is hard to say; the growing refusal to pay ship money from 1637 onwards did not bode well for it. But in that year a flash in Scotland lit the train that led to its destruction. An attempt to impose a Book of Common Prayer on their Kirk goaded the Scots into rebellion, and their National Covenant of 1638 was the oath of a nation to defend its fiercely cherished Presbyterian faith and worship. They swept away not only the Prayer Book but episcopacy itself, and when Charles prepared to meet defiance with force, they raised an army under Alexander Leslie, who drew hundreds of his fellow-veterans from the German wars to his banners. Charles's raw and half-hearted English troops advanced a few miles beyond the Tweed, met the Scots in battle array, and fled. A peace had to be patched up, leaving the tough and subtle Earl of Argyle, chief of the Covenanting lords, the real master of Scotland. But Charles was not accepting defeat, and now at last – too late – he recalled Wentworth from Ireland to take the helm at home.

Wentworth, now made Earl of Strafford, insisted that a Parliament should be called to pay for the large new army that was being raised. He believed he could manage it as he had managed a very different Parliament in Ireland. But it was John Pym who managed the Short Parliament when it met in April 1640, and not a penny would it vote until the stored-up grievances of fifteen years were redressed in full. After three weeks sitting it was dissolved, and Strafford told the Council that after its refusal of supplies 'the King is loose and absolved from all rules of government'. If tyranny was too strong a word for the last decade's fumbling parody of Tudor autocracy, it was apt enough for what now ensued. But it was not to last long; the fiasco of the Second Bishops' War finished it. The reluctant levies which were led to the northern border in the summer mutinied, deserted, broke open gaols, threw down enclosures, and made bonfires of the new communion-rails in the parish churches. Before this rabble of an army could strike, the Scots invaded and put it to disgraceful rout at Newburn on the Tyne. Charles again was forced to a truce; and this time the Scots were to remain in occupation of northern England, receiving £850 a day until a treaty was completed in London, where a new Parliament was to meet without delay.

The Long Parliament assembled on 3 November. Never had elections been fought so widely on political issues; never had the peers and gentry of the 'country interest' assembled with such confident purpose over the programme they meant to carry through. For the King could not dissolve them as he had dissolved the Short Parliament. Only their votes of supplies could hold the Scots north of the Tees, and pay the reduced English forces which still made a show of facing them. But with Strafford still at large, with two armies afoot on English soil, and a third raised for heaven knew what purpose in Ireland, with the London mob in a mood for bloody riots, it is no wonder that their proceedings were pitched in a high key, shot through even with moments of panic. Not that anyone seriously feared civil war in England. Why should they? The Scots were generally regarded as allies rather than enemies, and their presence as an opportunity to carry measures that would secure the subject's liberty and property for good. Pym seized it with both hands. The first step was to lodge Strafford in the Tower, impeached of high treason; Laud followed him there somewhat later. The story of how Strafford fought for his life before the Lords, and how Parliament, failing to pin its far-fetched charges of treason on him, brought him to the block by a tyrannous Act of Attainder, is one of the high tragedies of Stuart history. It might just have been averted, had not some royalist hotheads hatched a crazy plot to employ part of the English army in a *coup* against the Parliament, just when Strafford's fate hung in the balance. Strafford released the King from his promise to protect his life and fortune, and Charles sacrificed him in the hope of winning peace for his kingdom and saefty for his threatened Queen. He never forgave himself.

Before Strafford's head fell in May 1641, Parliament had already launched upon the great series of acts which was to bring the royal authority back within the bounds of 'fundamental law'. Having passed the Triennial Act to ensure frequent sessions in the future, it secured itself by another statute against being dissolved without its own consent. It abolished Star Chamber and the other prerogative courts, asserted its power over all customs dues and closed every loophole for non-parliamentary taxation from ship money downwards. By August the programme was complete, save for what needed to be done in the matter of religion. The alarms of the spring were dying down. The Scots withdrew across the Tweed in September; the Irish army was being disbanded and the English forces paid off as fast as money could be found. The men who had executed the King's government in the thirties were broken and scattered. There was a very welcome *détente,* and general hope for a fresh start on the basis of the good laws to which Charles had given his assent. Popular feeling had begun to warm towards him again. Unfortunately he chose this time to visit Scotland, with a dangerous idea in his mind of making a party for himself among the Scottish nobles. But Argyle could look after that, and the Parliament felt safe enough to treat itself to a six-weeks' recess.

It had still done nothing positive to settle its grievances over religion, for this question divided it deeply. Laud's policies had made Puritanism more militant than it had been since the middle of Elizabeth's reign, and had roused it to more uncompromising forms. But the thorough-going Puritans were no more than a large pressure group within a much broader opposition. They had failed during the summer to push through a bill to abolish the Church's episcopal government 'root and branch', and they faced a majority, even in the Commons, which would have no rough hands laid on the Book of Common Prayer. The Lords would not at present even remove the bishops from their own House, let alone abolish them. Parliament might – probably would – condemn Laudian innovations and transfer much of the initiative in ecclesiastical policy from the crown and the clergy to itself, but of a civil war over religion there was never the slightest prospect.

Then in October a catastrophe in Ireland darkened the whole sky. An explosion in Scotland had toppled the King's personal rule; now another in Ulster precipitated the crisis which led to civil war. The native inhabitants rose against the English and Scottish settlers who had expropriated their land. The movement grew rapidly into an organized national rebellion, and soon the entire area of English domination, from Londonderry down through Dublin and Cork, was in imminent danger of being overwhelmed. The slaughter was appalling; the numbers of Protestants slain or stripped naked to die of exposure rose into thousands. But the facts paled before the lurid and exaggerated reports which spread in England, and fanned the panic fear of popery to fever pitch. Worst of all, the leader of the Ulster rebels exhibited a forged commission from the King, authorizing him to seize the houses and lands of the Protestant settlers. Amid the horror and suspicion of that autumn, Charles's complicity was all too readily credited. Clearly an army must be raised to deal with the rebellion; but could the King be trusted with it?

So far, the moderate men of both Houses had been satisfied with the constitutional measures they had already passed. Pym and the more determined leaders of opposition were not; they distrusted Charles's good faith too deeply, and aimed at a more radical transfer of authority from crown to Parliament. Without the tragedy in Ireland, it is doubtful whether they could have carried the Houses with them. But now they exploited the atmosphere of crisis to press new demands – demands which crossed the frontier between reform and revolution. However far-reaching the acts already passed, government was still essentially the King's government, executed by servants chosen by him and responsible to him. But on 8 November Pym carried the Commons in a request to the King 'to employ only such counsellors and ministers as should be approved by his

Parliament'; if not, they would take the suppression of the Irish rebellion into their own hands.

Pym and his allies followed it up with the Grand Remonstrance, a tremendous, bitterly partisan indictment of fifteen years' misgovernment and a statement of radical plans for the future. Passionately debated for a fortnight, the Remonstrance was finally carried by a bare eleven votes in a session which ended at the unheard-of hour of 2 am, after fighting had all but broken out on the floor of the House. It was a narrow victory. Gone were the huge majorities which had passed the Triennial Act, condemned Strafford and abolished ship money and the prerogative courts. The united country interest of a year ago was united no longer. Men like Edward Hyde and Lord Falkland and Sir John Culpeper, who had voted with it hitherto, refused now to slip their sheet-anchor of ancient, fundamental law and launch out with Pym upon an unknown and revolutionary future. They and their like turned towards the King, variously moved by the deep-rooted English feeling for legality, devotion to the established religion and horror at the taint of rebellion. Common to them all, and perhaps deepest of all, was a fear of social revolution, whose spectre they saw in the rising turbulence of the London mob and the wild preachings of the extreme Puritan sects. On Pym's side, in contrast, was a conviction, strengthened by a mass of intrigue by both King and Queen, that if once Charles could possess himself of sufficient forces – English, Scottish, Irish, French, Spanish, it hardly mattered which – the laws to which he had so solemnly assented would not be worth the paper they were written on. The power to do mischief must therefore be taken from his hands.

Thus under the shadow of the Irish rebellion the royalist and parliamentarian parties began to define themselves. The issues became clearer in the next two months. One, Parliaments' bid to control the executive, was already starkly set forth. Equally crucial was Parliament's challenge to the King's sole right to dispose of the armed forces. No prerogative was vested more fundamentally in the crown; none seemed less safe with Charles I. The first proposal to usurp it from him came early in November from a rough-voiced but fervent back-bencher named Oliver Cromwell; then a month later the Militia Bill revealed the full extent of Parliament's claim to appoint the commanders of both the militia and the fleet. Over these two issues, above all others, the two sides finally divided. Religion was a powerful contributory factor, and coloured political attitudes and decisions to an extent scarcely conceivable today, but only a small minority of *dévots* on either side regarded it as the main quarrel between King and Parliament. By no means all Anglicans rallied to the King, and the parliamentarians were very far from being all Puritans. 'Religion was not a thing at first contested for', said Cromwell in retrospect, and such diverse figures as Richard Baxter, Colonel Hutchinson and Edward Hyde agreed with him.

Deeply as Parliament and nation were split by the end of 1641, war was not inevitable, or even widely expected. But before the New Year was a week old, Charles himself brought it very much nearer. Outraged by rumour that the Queen was to be impeached – arraigned, that is, by the Commons before the Lords for high crimes and misdemeanours – he caused his Attorney-General to launch an impeachment against six leaders of opposition: Lord Mandeville in the Upper House and Pym, Hampden, Haselrig, Holles and Strode in the Lower. Remove the ringleaders, he thought, and loyalty would have a chance to reassert itself. When the House failed to act promptly upon this extraordinary proceeding, Charles rode down to the Commons at the head of several hundred horsemen to arrest the five members himself. They were warned in time to escape by river, and all his rash show of force provoked was a far more impressive demonstration of armed strength by his opponents. The Commons took refuge in the City, which called out its militia; the Surrey trained bands too were mobilized, horsemen poured in from Hampden's Buckinghamshire, and all the mariners and lightermen on the Thames rose in support of the Parliament. On 10 January Charles slipped out of his capital by night with his wife and children, never to see it again till he was brought back a prisoner to be tried for his life.

Two very different kinds of counsel now contended for the King's ear. On the one hand were his courtiers and soldiers and the Queen's circle, who were ready to support any intrigue, any resort to force, any assistance whether English or foreign, Protestant or Papist, that would enable him to overthrow the 'rebels' and rule as he had done before. On the other were the moderates like Hyde and Falkland, newly won to his cause, and engaged to it only on the understanding that he sincerely renounced the practices of the thirties and accepted the 'new deal' of 1641. Upon such men, devoted to the rule of law and the historic Church of England, depended his chance of finding a party to sustain him and if need be an army to fight for him. Disastrously, he chose to speak with the voice of the latter group and act on the promptings of the former. This in the end made civil war inevitable. Even now, had he honestly renounced force and accepted the spirit of the Parliament's recent acts, had he stood forth as the true guardian of the ancient law and faith of England against demagogues and schismatics, Charles could have rallied the Lords and wrested back the narrow majority by which Pym commanded the Commons. Had he on the other hand trusted wholly to the desperate courses urged by the Queen and the hotheads, the inevitable show-down would have found him too isolated to fight.

Close as Charles strayed to the brink of war in January 1642, the immediate crisis passed. He was soon in negotiation with Parliament again, and guided by Hyde he now offered concessions in church and state which might have been the basis of a lasting settlement. He brought into his Council men like Falkland and Culpeper whom the Commons could trust, he offered hopes of compromise over a new Militia Bill, he even assented to an act excluding the bishops from the House of Lords. But Pym would have none of these olive-branches, and his reading of the King's intentions was all too sound. For Charles refused to return to Westminster, as both Houses begged him to; he pursued plans to secure Portsmouth and Hull as royalist strongholds; worse, he made it his main concern to get the Queen out of the country, not just for her own safety but to pawn the crown jewels and raise armed assistance in Holland and Denmark. When she had sailed he made his way to York, seeking in his northern capital a focus for the traditional loyalty which, he thought, only the noise of faction had drowned in his southern one.

By March all efforts at compromise over the militia had failed. The two Houses passed the Militia Bill as an ordinance, claiming for it the full force of law despite the King's refusal of his assent. This was to grasp at sovereignty; nothing could now bridge the gap between the two sides, and from now on the actions of both moved inexorably towards war. A stream of royalist peers, MPs and officials left Westminster for York, and Pym, who did not believe Charles could really fight, carried through Parliament in June a set of Nineteen Propositions which would have reduced the royal authority to a cipher. They also threatened radical changes in the Church's government and liturgy, for the secession of so many royalists had left for the first time a clear Puritan ascendancy at Westminster. Yet those who remained were not all zealots. There were many who shared the misgivings of the member who remarked to the Commons in July:

It is strange to note how we have insensibly slid into this beginning of a civil war, by one unexpected accident after another, as waves of the sea, which have brought us thus far; and we scarce know how, but from paper combats ... we are now come to the question of raising forces, and naming a General and officers of an army.

The Nineteen Propositions gave the King no choice but either to fight or surrender, and on 22 Angust he gave the formal signal for war by raising his standard at Nottingham. All over the country, local struggles were developing for the control of towns, strongholds, magazines and the militia or trained bands. Yet England faced the prospect of civil war with extreme reluctance. From Yorkshire and Cheshire down to Devon and Cornwall, there was a series of attempts at local treaties of neutrality whereby the gentry of both sides sought to keep war at least out of their own counties. All failed; and men of substance were forced to declare their allegiance (though not necessarily to fight) lest the King's party should treat them as rebels and the Parliament's as 'delinquents'. There were many would-be neutrals who nominally supported whichever side was in control where their estates lay, and many who changed sides as the fortunes of war shifted. Ties of family, of neighbourhood and of patronage between lord and client played large parts in the choice men made in 1642, and so did local feuds and rivalries. But in the main the choice was governed by the great political and religious issues which the last twelve months had raised, and these in hundreds of families divided father from son and brother from brother.

The motives which gave the King his supporters were on the whole simpler than the other side's. Deeply ingrained loyalty to crown and church, detestation of rebellion, family traditions of royal service, fortunes dependent on privileges or offices granted by the King, fear of mob rule – these are easily understood. Even so, there was always a difference in the royalist camp between the courtiers, who were simply for the King, right or wrong, against the rebels, and the constitutionalists like Hyde and Falkland whose ideal was not the old order of the thirties but the new one of 1641.

The parliamentarians' cause was the more complicated because they would never admit they were fighting the King. They had raised their army 'for the safety of the King's person, defence of both Houses of Parliament, and preserving of the true religion, the laws, liberty and peace of the kingdom', and its officers' commissions ran in the name of the King and Parliament. They clung to the fiction that they were only contending against the 'evil counsellors' who had seduced the King into breaking the old government by King, Lords and Commons, and most of them believed it. Pym had led them into demanding new powers for Parliament which would change the face of church and state. But how firmly they would stand to these demands when they found they had a long war

on their hands was an open question. There was always a
potential split between those who were contending deliberately
for parliamentary sovereignty and would fight till they got it,
and the more moderate and conservative men who had been
led to their present position by distrust of Charles and his
friends, but who feared the social consequences of civil war so
deeply that they would seek every opportunity to end it by a
negotiated peace. Pym, while he lived, held together a broad
middle-of-the-road majority and prevented Parliament from
flying apart into a war party and a peace party; but it was a
constant struggle, and only Pym could manage it.

The Civil War was not a class war. There was in a sense
a single ruling class in Stuart England, and it was now divided
from top to bottom. True, twice as many nobles sided with
the King as with the Parliament, but two-thirds of the 124
peers alive in 1640 owed their titles to Charles or his father.
True also, merchants tended to be parliamentarian unless they
profited directly from royal privileges, but that was to be
expected after all that their interests had suffered through the
crown's irresponsibility in mercantile policy, and with Puritanism so strong in the towns. But it was the landed gentry
who mattered most, in their collective wealth and social weight,
in Parliament and local government, and in their power to
raise their tenantry. From great magnates to petty squireens,
they were more than a hundred times as numerous as the
nobility, with whom their wealthiest members rubbed shoulders
on almost equal terms, and they had many points of contact
with the mercantile interest too. The gentry were not unevenly
divided between King and Parliament, and that is what made
the war so close a contest in its first two years.

About the smaller men, the copyholders and labourers and
craftsmen and shopkeepers who made up the larger part of the
population, it is impossible to generalize. At the lowest level
there must have been many fellows of that sturdy husbandman
who, when warned off Marston Moor because the King's and
the Parliament's armies were about to fight there, asked, 'What,

has them two fallen out then?' But interest in the great issues of the day spread far down through the social ranks, and where we do hear of popular demonstrations they were at the outset more often for Parliament rather than the King. Edward Hyde (writing later as Earl of Clarendon) was not the only royalist who felt the widespread hostility of what he called 'dirty people of no name'; indeed the sense that the lower orders were challenging the authority and privileges of their betters played a large part in turning men of quality towards the King.

If there was no clear social pattern in the choice of sides, there was certainly a rough geographical division. Support for Parliament was strongest south and east of an irregular line drawn from the Humber to the Severn, with important outposts in the cloth-making areas of the West Riding and Lancashire. Royalism predominated in the rest of the north, in Wales and the west midlands, and in the south-west peninsula. Parliament thus commanded the richer half of England, including all the wealth and resources of London, and had the advantage of interior lines. It meant that, if the King failed to win an early victory, time would be increasingly on the side of his opponents.

But wealth was not everything; military talent and experience counted for much too. Short as they were on both sides, the royalists had the advantage here for at least the first two years' campaigning. The very art of war, however, was largely forgotten in England. The last serious campaigns fought by English troops had been in Ireland, under Elizabeth; Buckingham's disastrous expeditions in the twenties had exposed the decrepitude of our military resources without doing a thing to remedy it. There was not even the nucleus of a standing army, and the trained bands of the counties were anything but trained. Few had even shot a musket at a target; their monthly muster-days in summer were devoted less to drill than to drinking and good fellowship. The only exceptions were the London trained bands, a proud body now 18,000 strong, well drilled and steady under fire, who saved the day for Parliament on more than one occasion. But they could not be used as regulars; a few weeks from home was the most they would stand.

Both sides enlisted volunteers easily enough at first; what both lacked were the experienced officers to train them. A fair number of gentlemen fancied themselves as soldiers because they had completed their education by going off to see an action or two in the German wars. More useful were the Englishmen and Scots who had served as professionals in the Dutch or Swedish or Spanish armies, but few as they were it was long before the best use was made of their skills. Many of those on the King's side were Roman Catholics, and to employ them too conspicuously was to play into the hands of enemy propaganda. But the main trouble was that both armies consisted initially of troops, companies and regiments raised by individual noblemen and gentlemen on their own initiative, from their own tenantry and neighbourhood, and often (mainly on the royalist side) at their own expense. These proud commanders regarded their units, which were often very small, very much as their own property, and they were none too willing to take orders or advice from professionals who were their social inferiors. They also generally failed to keep the gaps in their ranks filled with fresh recruits, so that there was a constant tendency for too many officers to be found commanding too few men. Parliament, with its power of the purse and its fuller authority, coped with this particular trouble better than the King ever could, but both sides shared the larger difficulty of subordinating social prestige to military competence.

Discipline was deplorable on both sides in the early stages. Most of the rank-and-file enlisted for pay, excitement and plunder, without much thought of long and hard service. Lack of pay soon led to indiscriminate pillaging, and this in turn to contempt for orders and general demoralization. The farther the men marched from their homes the more unreliable they became. Parliament had as yet few regiments like John Hampden's greencoats, who sang psalms on the march, abstained from plunder, and heard a sermon twice a week from their chaplain William Spurstowe. Elsewhere in Essex's army we hear of regiments fighting each other for their loot, cavalry plundering infantry and infantry robbing their own officers. If few battles were well fought in the first year or two, not all the blame should fall on the generals, who had to deal with sub-ordinates who obeyed orders if they liked them and soldiers whose morale was as uncertain as their training was inadequate. Not until the New Model learnt its trade in 1645 did a Civil War army approach the elaboration of drill, and hence the refinement in tactics, which had become characteristic of the professional armies of the Continent during the last two gen-erations. It was for the most part a very amateur war. Deser-tion was a constant problem; at the end of the first winter Essex's army had shrunk to a third of its original size and needed drastic reorganization. The King's forces suffered less than this, for his cavalry was largely composed of men of means, while the many Welshmen among his infantry, being drawn from a hard, poor and distant country, had less tempta-tion to make for home when pay failed or conditions became tough.

Of the chief commanders, the Earl of Essex, the Parlia-ment's Lord General, has already been introduced. Charles had lost his first General-in-Chief at Edgehill; his second, Patrick Ruthven, Earl of Forth, was a competent enough pro-fessional from the Swedish service, but was now about seventy years old. Forth's authority was weakened by Prince Rupert's claim as General of the Horse to an independent command, and Rupert, besides being the King's nephew, was a very con-siderable soldier. Even though his experience in the German wars had been cut short by capture before his nineteenth birth-day, he could lead cavalry like a man possessed, he knew his siege-craft, and in the storming of fortified towns he had no equal. Beyond that, however, he never showed that he had the comprehensive grasp to direct a full-scale battle, and in action the hot blood of his twenty-three years was apt to blind him to everything but his immediate objective. Honthorst's portrait conveys something of the dark fire of the man; the curl of the lip hints at contempt for courtly hyperbole and courtly incompetence. Unfortunately, in the King's councils of war soldiers needed all the tact they could muster if their advice was to prevail over that of mere courtiers.

Memorial Medal to the Earl of Essex, 1646

2

The War Takes Shape

THE FIRST CAMPAIGN of the two main armies, which culminated in the drawn battle of Edgehill and petered out after the check to the King's advance on London at Turnham Green, ended in a large question mark: would the war go on? King Charles was more than ever determined not to bow to terms which would deprive him of his sovereignty; King Pym was not shaken in his purpose of transferring effective sovereignty to the Parliament. But between these two inflexible wills, many lesser ones wavered. At Westminster especially there was deep disquiet at the prospect of a long and wasting war, at the social anarchy it might unloose, and at the taint of treason in endangering the King's very person. Only six weeks after Turnham Green the fickle London crowds were filling Palace Yard and crying 'Peace! peace!' Pym knew there was no bridge between the King's ends and his own, short of surrender by one or the other, but the large peace party in both Houses had to be given its head. And so a desultory, futile negotiation was carried on at Oxford from January to April 1643, on terms much milder than those of the Nineteen Propositions, but still much too stiff for success. Charles was vastly stronger now than last summer, and he looked forward to clear victory in the coming year. To ask him to abolish episcopacy, disband his forces, hand over control of the militia and abandon his most faithful supporters to Parliament's 'justice' was a waste of time.

But Pym could use the lull to push through the measures which he knew were vital for the campaigns to come. A whole new administration had to be improvised, for very many officials of the Exchequer and of every other office of government had sided with the King. Regular taxation had to replace the loans and voluntary contributions which had sustained Essex's army so far; the 'weekly pay', levied at unprecedented rates on all classes of society, was the main device. Another problem was to organize the local management of the war effort. To look after local defence, recruiting, arms, quarters, provisions and so on, a system of county committees was erected, each consisting of the richest and most active parliamentary gentry in the shire. Some counties were grouped in associations, of which one, the Eastern Association, raised a force which was to develop into a new field army to rival Essex's. The germ of a third field army, based mainly on the forces of Bristol and Gloucester, could be seen in the Western Association, which Sir William Waller was sent to command in February.

Neither side could afford to put all its resources into a single army. Control of territory was almost more important than the winning of battles in these early stages, for each side's power to raise taxes, recruits, supplies and munitions could be roughly measured by the sheer acreage it commanded. Hence the rash of local garrisons and the whole series of small local armies, additional to those under the direct authority of the commanders-in-chief, which make the military picture so complicated. Some of these local forces must be mentioned, however, for they will play a significant part in the story of the major battles. Moreover they were little affected by the truce which quieted the two main armies during the abortive Treaty of Oxford.

In Yorkshire, the great port of Hull was held for the Parliament, and a gallant little force, raised mainly from the West Riding towns by Ferdinando, Lord Fairfax and his son Sir Thomas, was defying the royalist army of 8000 which the Earl of Newcastle had brought down from the north-east. Sir Thomas's brilliant capture of Leeds in January and Wakefield in May showed what could be done against superior numbers, but the odds were too long for his success to last. In Lancashire another great magnate, the Earl of Derby, raised a minor army for the King, to challenge the cluster of Puritan towns which centred on Manchester. But Cheshire was held for the Parliament by a soldier of talent and spirit, Sir William Brereton: and in April, Derby's disorderly levies were routed for good near Whalley by a regiment or two of local cavalry and a band of angry countrymen who had hastily gathered to defend their homes. Things went better for Charles in the midlands. Newcastle's cavalry swept down in December to seize the vital key-point of Newark, and when in the next two months Ashby-de-la-Zouch, Tamworth, Lichfield and Stafford fell to the royalists, the Parliament's life-line between north and south looked like being strangled. Southward along the lower Severn, however, Waller was soon earning himself the name of 'William the Conqueror', thrusting out in March and April to take Malmesbury on one side and Hereford on the other. Across the Bristol Channel, Parliament's hold on Somerset, Devon and Dorset depended on its garrisons in the principal towns and ports, for most of the gentry were royalist. Cornwall was wholly the King's, and the hard-fighting Cornish levies had a brilliant leader in Sir Ralph Hopton. Their victory at Braddock Down in January gave the western roundheads a sharp taste of their quality.

The Parliament's main campaign began well in April when Essex advanced towards Oxford and captured Reading. But that was his last success for many months, for camp fever (probably typhoid) now wasted his army, made all too vulnerable by the filth and overcrowding of its quarters. The tide turned fully in the King's favour in May, when Hopton at Stratton routed the Parliament's western forces, double his own in strength, and advanced unchecked through Devon into Somerset to meet a considerable force which Charles had sent westward under the Marquis of Hertford. With it was Prince Maurice, Rupert's brother. Waller was called southwards to the rescue, but not in time to prevent Hopton and Hertford from joining forces at Chard.

This was the first move in a grand strategy which was to bring the King nearer to victory in 1643 than he would ever come again. The plan was for a threefold advance on London. One prong was to consist of this combined western army, advancing through the southern counties and striking at the capital from below. Newcastle's northerners were to form another, thrusting directly southward. Charles's own army, based on Oxford, would hold Essex's engaged and deliver its own blow from the west when the time came.

June and July, during which this plan developed, were months of disaster for the Parliament. When Essex dragged his disease-wasted army forward from Reading against Oxford, Rupert broke up its advance with a devastating two-day cavalry raid, in resisting which John Hampden fell mortally wounded on Chalgrove Field. It was little more than a skirmish, but it cost Pym his best ally, and Parliament the *preux chevalier* of its cause. In Yorkshire, Newcastle brought the Fairfaxes' little army to battle against almost overwhelming odds at Adwalton Moor, and broke it utterly. The Fairfaxes had to abandon the West Riding and lead their shattered remnants through severe hazards to Hull – and Hull was only just saved in time from being betrayed by its Governor to the King. News just as bad soon followed from the west. The Cornishmen staggered Waller in an action on Lansdown Hill near Bath which for sheer dash and endurance has few parallels in the Civil War. But Waller had only been checked, and when he succeeded in cooping up the royalists in Devizes he counted on destroying them. Prince Maurice, however, was given time to dash to Oxford for cavalry reinforcements, and in the bloody battle of Roundway Down on 13 July it was Waller's army that was destroyed. Hard on this disaster, London itself was threatened for nearly a week by a royalist rising in Kent. Catastrophe reached its climax on the 26th when Rupert stormed and captured Bristol, the second port in the kingdom and the greatest Parliamentary stronghold in the west. After this the garrisons in Dorset fell one after another, until only Lyme and Poole held out.

City and Parliament reeled under these blows. A finely fought cavalry action by Oliver Cromwell failed to prevent Newcastle from taking Gainsborough, and soon all Lincolnshire was lost. The rich territory of the Eastern Association was directly threatened. Colonel Cromwell had become a leading spirit in that Association; he had increased the single troop of horse with which he had entered the war into a double regiment, the flower of many fine cavalry units raised from the tough, independent yeomen and freeholders of Puritan East Anglia. But cavalry was not enough. Cromwell called the authorities at Cambridge to action:

> It's no longer disputing, but out instantly all you can. Raise all your [trained] bands; send them to Huntingdon; get up what volunteers you can; hasten your horses . . . I beseech you spare not, but be expeditious and industrious. Almost all our foot have quitted Stamford; there is nothing to interrupt an enemy but our horse that is considerable. You must act lively; do it without distraction. Neglect no means.

That was one reaction. But at Westminster all was conflict, recrimination and clamour for peace, for from late in June through most of July Pym quite lost control of the Parliament. It was one of the great crises of the war. The peace party, strong in the Commons, entirely dominated the Lords for a time, and looked to Essex for support. The war party in the Commons and the City made a scapegoat of Essex and pressed for a new army, to be commanded by Waller. Essex himself wavered. He tried to resign, then offered the Lords the extraordinary advice that peace terms like those that had failed last winter should be offered once more, and that if the King rejected them he should be asked to withdraw from the field so that the two armies could engage in a formal and final trial by battle. But when the Lords adopted peace propositions that amounted to surrender, Pym persuaded Essex to refuse his support to them. In London, sermons, mass demonstrations and a strong petition from the City fathers protested against the spirit of defeatism. Essex was assured that his own army would be recruited, and was induced to commission Waller to command a new one of 11,000 men, to be raised by the City. At the same time, the Earl of Manchester, formerly the Lord Mandeville whom Charles had tried to impeach, was made Major-General of the Eastern Association's army, whose infantry strength was to be raised to 10,000. Parliament was committed now to fighting on, and Pym was in control again. Having beaten the pacifists, he now took the chance to curb the more dangerous spirits of the war party. When Henry Marten suggested to the Commons 'that it were better one family should be destroyed than many', and admitted that the family he meant was the King's, the House at Pym's instance expelled him and sent him to the Tower.

By August the King's grand strategy was already revealing its weaknesses. It was never easy to persuade local levies like Newcastle's and Hopton's to campaign far from their homes, and when those homes were threatened by an army in the rear it was impossible. In the north Hull still held out, and from its walls Sir Thomas Fairfax's cavalry was soon making such damaging forays that Newcastle decided he must return and besiege it before he could attempt any further advance. As for the army in the west, the fear that it would march straight on London proved groundless. Plymouth, Exeter and other parliamentary garrisons held out strongly behind it, and so above all did Gloucester, defiant in a vast area now solidly royalist, and impeding access to the great royalist recruiting-ground of south Wales. So the King made Gloucester his next objective, while Prince Maurice was detached to complete the conquest of the south-west.

Through the late summer, the King's hopes and the Parliament's fears hung on these two sieges of Hull and Gloucester – on Gloucester's fate especially. Charles summoned the city in person on 10 August, confident that Colonel Massey, its young Governor, was no enemy to him and would deliver it into his hands. But Massey bade him defiance, and Pym, mortally sick though he now was, called up the flagging spirits of the Parliament and brought it back to a sense of common purpose. Essex and London rose to the occasion. Recruits for the army poured in, the shutters went up on the shops so that apprentices and journeymen could go out and fight, and six City trained band regiments prepared for sterner service than at Turnham Green. On the 26th Essex marched out with 15,000 men, borne on a new wave of confidence and resolution. Ten days later they raised the siege of Gloucester, when its defenders were down to their last three barrels of powder. It was too early to triumph, however, for Maurice was knocking away the Parliament's footholds in Devon one by one, and Essex, so far from being able to relieve them, could only think of getting his makeshift, hungry army back to London without being mauled by Rupert's and the King's main forces. Rupert barred his way at Newbury and forced him to give battle on 20 September. A fierce and confused fight it was, with the trained bands contesting every hedge of the thick enclosures south-west of the town. It ended indecisively, but heavy losses and shortage of ammunition forced the royalists to retreat next day towards Oxford, and despite some harassing by Rupert's cavalry Essex was able to lead his tired, battered forces safely back to London. He deserved the ovation he received there, after the carping criticism he had borne all summer. He had fought his best campaign, and given heart to his cause when it was most needed.

Hull too was delivered; indeed, being open to relief from the sea, Newcastle's half-hearted siege operations never seriously threatened it. Late in September, Sir Thomas Fairfax ferried his cavalry (which was useless in a beleagured town) over the Humber to join Cromwell's in Lincolnshire. It was the beginning of a great partnership. Together they routed the royalist cavalry of the midlands, twice their own in strength, near Winceby on 11 October, and soon the rest of Lincolnshire was recovered. The day after Winceby, Newcastle raised the siege of Hull, his forces already halved by hunger, desertion and the fire of the defenders. The threat from the north evaporated; indeed it was from the north that Parliament now looked for relief, and beyond relief victory.

This was because Pym had led his party into the momentous step of calling in the Scots. Pym had wanted them as allies almost since the war started, and the first appeal to them had been sent just before Turnham Green. But though the interest of both countries cooled as that first crisis passed, the second, in July, caused the Scots themselves to reopen the question.

Argyle not only realized that if the Parliament were beaten his own country's turn would come next, he knew from captured letters that Charles was already planning to induce the Catholic Irish of Ulster to invade Scotland. Parliament needed little persuading, and on 7 August Sir Henry Vane the younger reached Edinburgh with a group of fellow-commissioners to negotiate the pact. They had no easy task, for the two kingdoms differed in their objects. Whereas England merely wanted a Scottish army, the Scots demanded a religious covenant, similar to their own of four years earlier, which would pledge England to a Presbyterian national church like theirs. Now, although Parliament had already voted to abolish bishops and summoned an Assembly of Divines to advise it on the reformation of religion, it had no wish to bind England to a rigid Scottish Presbytery. Vane himself, like Cromwell, represented a strain of Puritanism well to the left of Presbyterianism, whose intolerant spirit would leave no room for him and his kind. But common needs spurred the treaty forward, and the Solemn League and Covenant was concluded after only ten days' negotiation. It was far more than a treaty between states; it was a solemn oath to be sworn by every adult male in both kingdoms, which were to be 'conjoined in a firm peace and union to all posterity'. It promised the reformation of the Churches of England and Ireland according to the model of the Scottish Kirk, though Vane secured a verbal loophole which might mitigate the narrow conformity that this suggested. It vowed to preserve not only 'the rights and privileges of the Parliaments' but 'the King's Majesty's person and authority', though his chief supporters were to be tried and punished as 'incendiaries, malignants or evil instruments'. This strange document ended in a solemn act of repentance for the sins of the two kingdoms which had brought them to their present pass. It was followed in due course by a military treaty, whereby an army of 20,000 Scots was to serve in England at the rate of £100,000 down and £30,000 a month.

On 25 September the Commons and the Assembly of Divines swore to the Covenant in the church which they now,

for fear of idolatry, called simply 'Margaret's Westminster'.
Ten days earlier the King had concluded a very different pact.
While his enemies trafficked with the Scots, he had turned to
Ireland, where a Roman Catholic Confederacy now ruled nine-
tenths of the land. After months of negotiation, the Marquis
of Ormonde now signed in his name a truce known as the Cessation, which left the Confederates in recognized possession of
all that their rebellion had won. It released the meagre English
forces which had been struggling against the Irish so that they
could fight for the King in England, and the Confederacy
agreed to send £30,000 towards their upkeep. It brought him
no native Irish forces, though he hoped keenly that they would
follow, and spent the rest of the war (and longer) angling for
them. English national pride and hatred of popery being what
they were, the Cessation did him more harm than its slender
military value proved to be worth.

The year's shocks were not over for the Parliament when
Gloucester and Hull were saved. Essex's weakened army lost
Reading early in October, while Maurice took Dartmouth and
threatened Plymouth. And when a strong sortie from Oxford
threw a garrison into Newport Pagnell, astride London's sup-
ply lines from the midlands, Essex had to conduct yet another
rescue operation with the help of the City trained bands.
Finally, Hopton advanced through Hampshire and Sussex in
December and captured Arundel before the tide of his success
began to ebb. Waller at first was powerless to stop him, for
his City lads decided they had had enough of field service and
made off home.

The year 1643 ended with the Parliament's armies in
wretched shape. Voting large new levies was much easier than
keeping them paid, equipped and supplied, and persuading
them to serve wherever they were called. The flow of volunteers had dried up, and foot soldiers had to be found now by
impressment. The armies of Essex, Waller and Manchester
were not so much partners as jealous rivals for the Parliament's
limited resources in money, men and munitions; the recruitment of one merely led to desertions from the others, whose

soldiers would slip off to re-enlist where pay and conditions of service looked more promising.

The year had been decidedly the King's. His gains in territory and garrisons had been large, especially in the south and south-west; he had kept his enemies almost continually on the defensive, and they had yet to win a major battle. But sanguine as he was, he had just not come near enough to full success, and time was turning more heavily against him than he knew.

The King's victories in the summer might have broken the Parliament's will to fight had it not been for Pym. And now the Parliament suffered its greatest loss of the year, for on 8 December Pym died of cancer. This dedicated man, so cool and patient in political manœuvre yet so passionately engaged, so little known beyond his public acts and so single-minded in those, has a larger claim to be the architect of the Parliament's eventual victory than any of its generals. Except at rare moments, he had prevented it from splitting irreconcilably between a peace party and a war party. After his death the split widened ominously, for the younger Vane and Oliver St John, the war party's leaders, cared less for persuading their more cautious colleagues than for out-manœuvring them. An early instance arose when a new executive was set up to direct the conduct of the war in the coming year. This, the Committee of Both Kingdoms, was made necessary by the Scottish alliance. It was composed of some seven peers, fourteen MPs and four commissioners from Scotland. Vane and his friends determined its composition beforehand and pushed, edged and juggled it through Parliament during a fortnight of fierce political infighting. They got what they wanted, which was a genuine executive which could take military decisions without referring everything to the two Houses, and they saw to it that the half-dozen peace-party men who had to be included would be easily out-voted. They brought in Cromwell, and they managed to exclude Denzil Holles, the peace party's leader in the Commons. It was cleverly handled, but it was not the sort of success that would be easily forgiven.

The story of the 1644 campaigns, which were to culminate in the clash of five armies on a field near York in the biggest and bloodiest battle ever fought on English soil, begins on a bitter January day with the crossing of the Tweed by 21,000 Scotsmen. This army of the Covenant marched under orders which breathed the conviction that it was about the Lord's business. Each regiment was to have its minister and lay elders, forming a kirk-session like that of every Scottish parish, and besides morning and evening prayers daily there were to be sermons both morning and afternoon on the Lord's Day. Soldiers who swore or profaned the Sabbath must make 'public repentance in the midst of the congregation', besides incurring loss of pay and detention. Whores found following the camp were threatened with death if they were married women, and if they were single the hangman was to marry them forthwith (presumably to whoever was found consorting with them) and then scourge them out of the army. Death was the penalty for plundering, rape or drunkenness on guard; irreverent speech against the King or his authority was to be punished as treason. All were enjoined to 'live together as friends and brethren' and abstain from the quarrels which might provoke duels.

The general of this blue-bonneted host was Alexander Leslie, Earl of Leven. Stumpy, paunchy, homely of speech and almost illiterate, the authority he wielded over the Scottish nobles in military matters rested on thirty years in the Swedish service, Europe's finest school of war. He had won a knighthood from the great Gustavus Adolphus and risen to the rank of Field-Marshal. He had routed the English at Newburn; now he had the rare assignment of leading a Scottish army to fight on English soil with Englishmen as allies. Dogged, unspectacular and now well over sixty years old, he already had an old man's reluctance for unnecessary exertions. In the endless Continental warfare which had taught him his trade, brilliance in strategy and tactics often counted for less than the sheer craft of raising, arming and training armies, feeding them off the country, and instilling the discipline of their strange, hard communal lives so that disease and desertion should not take a heavier toll of them than the actual fighting. There was more fire and dash in his General of the Horse, David Leslie – not a kinsman, but schooled like him in the armies of Gustavus.

Heavy snow and floods slowed the Scots' advance during this severe and protracted winter. Leven attempted an assault on Newcastle on 3 February, but the Marquis of Newcastle (as he now was) had arrived back just in time to stiffen the town's resistance, and the Scots were sharply repulsed. London had to give up its hopes that its sorely missed supplies of sea-coal from the Tyne would be released in time to save it from shivering through the rest of the winter. A lull of three weeks followed before a break in the weather encouraged Leven to push on across the Tyne, leaving six foot regiments to blockade the town of Newcastle. March passed without a battle, though the Marquis tried more than once to bring one on, and the month ended with the Scots still based on Sunderland and the royalists on Durham. It was desultory campaigning, but the conditions were very hard, and both sides, Newcastle's cavalry especially, were suffering from them. The Scots often went hungry through the attacks on their foraging parties by the royalist horse, but it is doubtful whether either army had so much to bear as the wretchedly poor countryside which both of them wasted and pillaged.

No greater contrast could be imagined between two generals than existed between Leven and Newcastle. The Marquis was the sort of *grand seigneur* to whom the professional parts of soldiering – all that Leven was master of – were rather below a nobleman's dignity. They were looked after by his Lieutenant-General, James King, another Scottish veteran of the Swedish service whom Charles had recently ennobled as Lord Eythin. Yet Newcastle had been a natural choice for the generalship of the north. His vast wealth, his social status, his fine presence and exquisite courtesy had given him an authority over the local gentry and a power to raise men that no other northern magnate could have rivalled. No one bore better the dignity of a general, or exposed himself in action with a cooler courage. Unfortunately a military situation was developing which called for more than sang-froid and *comme il faut*. To be fair, he had taken up this burden not because he cared for it but out of a chivalrous loyalty to the King in his distress. He was pouring a vast fortune into the royal cause. But he was also defending a whole order of things that involved his own survival as well as his master's. 'He loved monarchy', wrote Clarendon, 'as it was the foundation and support of his own greatness; and the Church, as it was well constituted for the splendour and security of the crown; and religion, as it cherished and maintained that order and obedience that was necessary to both.' His great passion was horsemanship, but otherwise his tastes were more literary than warlike. He aspired as a poet and a playwright; James Shirley had helped him with his plays, as Dryden was to do later. Ben Jonson had written masques for his entertainments, Thomas Hobbes enjoyed his friendship and generosity, and a poet, Sir William Davenant, now served him as general of artillery. He carried a certain romantic bravura into his public life; his grand gestures and his cult of the dramatic and fantastical bore the stamp of the baroque. A year ago, when the Fairfaxes had been outwitting him with their inferior forces, he had published a challenge to them to follow 'the example of our heroic ancestors, who used not to spend their time in scratching one another out of holes, but in pitched fields determined their doubts'; to which Lord Fairfax replied with an understandable refusal 'to follow the rules of Amadis de Gaule, or the Knight of the Sun'.

While Leven and Newcastle sparred ineffectually at each other across the northern snows, the war was not standing still elsewhere. Lord Byron had recently been shaping a new royal army in Cheshire, largely from troops released from service in Ireland by the Cessation and landed at Chester. In January Sir Thomas Fairfax took his Yorkshire cavalry to help Sir William Brereton deal with it, and together they beat it resoundingly at Nantwich. About 1500 of the men from Ireland were taken prisoners, and half of them promptly enlisted with their captors. Meanwhile Lord Fairfax made steady progress in the East Riding. A still sharper threat to the King's hold on the north developed early in March when Sir John Meldrum assembled over 6000 local parliamentary troops and laid siege to Newark. That was one place Charles dared not lose. Rupert was at Shrewsbury, tackling the heavy duties lately placed upon him as President of Wales, when he got orders to go to its relief. He made the march in eight days, picking up what local forces he could on the way. On his arrival he fought such a brilliant cavalry action that he soon had Newark's besiegers helplessly besieged, and Meldrum had to surrender with the loss of all his arms and artillery. Shorn of their defenders, Gainsborough, Lincoln, Sleaford and Crowland soon fell back into royalist hands.

Rupert had soon to restore his borrowed troops to their garrisons and return to Shrewsbury, but he had upset all Parliament's plans, and badly shaken its morale. Essex was alerted to protect London, while the royalist hold on Lincolnshire tied down Manchester to the defence of the Eastern Association. A motion in the Commons to approach the King once more for peace, without the Scots' concurrence, was only defeated by the Speaker's casting vote. An hour or so later, to shame this disgraceful proposal, came news of Waller's timely victory over the Earl of Forth at Cheriton on 29 March. With Forth on that unlucky field was Hopton and his forces, who were now recalled to Oxford to be absorbed in the King's main field army. It was the only one Charles now had in the south, apart from 6000 men under Maurice who were bogged down in a slow and wasteful siege of Lyme. The initiative passed to the parliamentarians, and Waller began to threaten Dorset.

In April the war in the north really got moving. From Cheshire Sir Thomas Fairfax had sent back young Colonel Lambert to set about recovering the West Riding towns, and the work was going well. Sir Thomas followed him soon after, bringing about 1500 Lancashire foot as well as his own cavalry, and when he rejoined his father and Lambert before Selby their combined forces totalled over 5000. Selby held a strong garrison, but it was no match for the skill and fire with which the Fairfaxes stormed the town on 11 April. The Scots were on the march too. They had come within two miles of Durham, and Newcastle, threatened in front and rear, withdrew hurriedly to York with Leven on his tail. The Fairfaxes met the Scots near Wetherby on the 20th, and two days later their combined forces, about 20,000 strong, sat down before York. They were still too few to invest its extensive walls fully, and Fairfax wrote to urge that Manchester's Eastern Association army should be sent at once to help them clinch their splendid advantage. Newcastle sent away most of his cavalry under Sir Charles Lucas to Newark, where it could be more useful, and appealed urgently to the King for relief. He had no more than 5000 foot to defend the city, apart from such citizens as he could press into the service.

York would not fall suddenly, but it counted for so much, and the threat to it was so severe, that the north not only became quite suddenly the main theatre of war but looked as if it might be the scene of the war's decisive battle. If York should fall and Newcastle's army surrender, Charles would assuredly lose most of England north of Trent, a vast recruiting-ground and an indispensable source of contributions to his war-chest. He must keep his footholds there until he could land fresh forces from Ireland; he must keep the way open between his two kingdoms in case the young Marquis of Montrose should succeed in his plans for setting Scotland on fire. The relief of York was an obvious task for Rupert, who was busy at Shrewsbury licking a small army into shape out of some fresh Welsh levies and some more troops from Ireland. But could he be spared? The King himself might be in danger. When Charles took the field in April he had only about 10,000 men. Parliament might concentrate both Essex's and Waller's armies against him, and perhaps Manchester's too, while Massey and the Gloucester garrison were becoming uncomfortably aggressive in the lower Severn. Fortunately for Charles, Essex was for the moment very short of men and money, Waller had been halted once more because his London trained bands made off home, while Manchester would not leave the Eastern Association so long as the royalists dominated Lincolnshire.

Nevertheless, Charles felt sufficiently threatened to summon Rupert and all his forces to Oxford.

Rupert sent Lord Byron to remonstrate, then visited Oxford himself at the end of April. He arranged a sensible defensive strategy for Charles and the Oxford forces which should secure them adequately while he himself marched to save the north and his brother Maurice pressed on in the west. The King's infantry was to be distributed between the garrisons of Oxford, Reading, Wallingford, Abingdon and Banbury; some of his cavalry was to be kept as a mobile force to relieve any one of them that might be attacked, while the rest went to reinforce Maurice.

The month of May soon showed how right Rupert was to put York first. On the 6th Manchester stormed Lincoln, and at once sent the fine Eastern Association cavalry under Cromwell, now his Lieutenant-General, to support the Scots and the Fairfaxes. Already he had orders to follow with the rest of his army and join the siege. But as Manchester set his course for York, so did Rupert. The Prince left Shrewsbury on the 16th with only 8000 men, three-quarters of them infantry. His famous 'York March' could not head straight for York, however, for he had to pick up reinforcements on the way, and there were tasks which claimed him in Lancashire. His cavalry strength became more respectable when he collected Byron's forces from Chester. His army captured and plundered Stockport on 25 May, thereby relieving Lathom House, where for many months the Countess of Derby had been defending the last royalist island in Lancashire. Her besiegers withdrew to Bolton, but Bolton's turn came three days later, and the manner of its taking brought a whiff of the German wars in which Rupert had been nurtured. Only 700 of its defenders were granted quarter, after 1600 had been slain, and the town was given over to sack. At Bury the Prince was joined by George Goring, who brought with him Lucas and the cavalry regiments which Newcastle had sent out of York. Lancashire, which like Yorkshire was a county of sharply divided allegiance, was beginning to respond to Rupert's successes. The streets of Wigan were strewn with flowers and spring-green branches for him when he rode in, and the Earl of Derby was raising recruits in large numbers. Liverpool was the next objective, to secure another landing-place for troops from Ireland; but Liverpool's mud walls, padded with bags of wool and grimly manned, withstood five days' bombardment and more than one assault before it too became a scene of slaughter and plunder.

The next eight days Rupert spent between Liverpool and Lathom, modelling his patchwork army, absorbing his new recruits and pondering his next move. He would have liked to complete the conquest of Lancashire by humbling Manchester, before marching on York with every company the north could furnish. But he was disquieted by news from the south which fully justified his angry distrust of the men about the King. Old Forth, now Earl of Brentford, had grown gouty, bibulous, deaf and very slow; Lord Wilmot, General of the Horse, and Lord Henry Percy, General of the Ordnance, were untrustworthy intriguers; Hopton and Sir Jacob Astley were honest soldiers, but less glib and persuasive in councils of war than Lord Digby, the Secretary of State, who was ready to seize every chance of undermining Rupert's authority. Between them they had persuaded Charles to withdraw his garrisons from Reading and Abingdon, to give his army more mobility. Essex and Waller gratefully occupied both towns and closed in on Oxford from east and west. To avoid the trap, Charles had to move out in a hurry on 2 June with only 3000 horse and fewer foot. He got to Evesham with Waller and Essex both on his tracks and evidently about to join forces. Only a dozen miles away Massey had just taken Tewkesbury, and more parliamentary forces were moving southward from Shropshire to meet him. Charles spent some days of agonized hesitation at Worcester, then headed north for Bewdley with no better hope than to seek refuge with Rupert in Lancashire. As Digby admitted, 'had Essex and Waller either pursued us or attacked Oxford, we had been lost'.

But Charles was saved by Essex's folly. At a council of war

at Stow-on-the-Wold on the 6th, Essex, against all protests, ordered Waller to continue the pursuit alone while he himself marched off to relieve Lyme and recover the west. When a shocked Committee of Both Kingdoms tried to recall him, Essex merely sent back a petulant protest, claiming to judge the situation best for himself and order his subordinate Waller as he thought fit. Charles soon felt safer, and from Bewdley he wrote a letter to Rupert on the 14th which in a sense precipitated the battle of Marston Moor. The Prince is said to have carried it on him to his dying day.

> If York be lost [Charles wrote] I shall esteem my crown little less [than lost], unless supported by your sudden march to me, and a miraculous conquest in the south before the effects of the northern power can be found here; but if York be relieved, and you beat the rebels' armies of both kingdoms which were before it – then, but otherwise not, I may possibly make a shift upon the defensive to spin out time until you come to assist me; wherefore I command and conjure you . . . that, all new enterprises laid aside, you immediately march according to your first intention, with all your force, to the relief of York; but if that be either lost or have freed themselves from the besiegers, or that for want of powder you cannot undertake that work, that you immediately march with your whole strength to Worcester, to assist me and my army.

Involved as this letter was, it could only bear one meaning to Rupert; unless York had already fallen or been freed, or he had too little powder to succour it, he was to march there at once, not only to relieve the city but to fight its besiegers and beat them.

The investment of York was complete when Manchester arrived there with the main body of his army on 3 June. He covered the north side, while Leven took the west and south-west and Fairfax the east and south-east. The three generals resisted appeal after appeal from Westminster to send strong forces to the relief of Lancashire; Vane himself came to their camp to press the point, but they convinced him that they were right. Within the walls Newcastle and Eythin had taken all provisions into a common store, put soldiers and civilians on to a strict ration and limited all alike to one meal a day. The siege guns were playing now, and the fight for the suburbs was on. The defenders were sallying out to burn down the streets and houses outside the walls, to prevent the besiegers from gaining a covered approach by channelling through them. Newcastle protested at their breach of etiquette in proceeding so far without delivering a formal summons. He got one on the 12th, but though he gained a few days' respite for negotiation, he felt obliged to reject the three generals' terms on the 15th. Next day he had to withstand the first assault. Mines had been planted below three widely separated sections of the wall, the plan being to explode them simultaneously so that the three armies could storm in from their several quarters. But whether through a sudden danger of his tunnel flooding or a jealous desire to engross all the credit, Manchester's fiery Major-General, Lawrence Crawford, sprang his mine prematurely. It made a fair breach, and his men fought their way through it into the streets. But since neither the Scots nor Fairfax knew of their predicament in time to divert the garrison from bringing its whole strength against them, they were eventually driven out with the loss of two or three hundred men.

Three days later Rupert set out from Lathom on the last swift stages of his march to the city's relief. The King's letter ended all his hesitations; fast though recruits were coming in, he must take what strength he already had. What made him hasten was not so much that York might fall within a fortnight as that the King was still in danger, and needed his help in the south. He could not know that Charles had retreated quite safely to Woodstock, collected reinforcements from Oxford, and was now about to appear at Buckingham, threatening the almost undefended eastern counties with 5000 horse and as many foot. There was a fine flurry of alarm at Westminster, where it was feared he might descend on London itself. Unfortunately Charles hesitated too long over his next move and gave Waller time to catch up with him. But in the untidy action that was fought at Cropredy Bridge on the Cherwell on the 29th, Waller came off the worst, and mutiny and desertion prevented him from trying another throw with the King. By the time Rupert approached York Charles was on his way back to Evesham, having turned the tables on his assailants to an extent that three weeks earlier would have seemed unimaginable.

£3 Gold Piece of Charles I
coined at Oxford, 1643

3

Marston Moor

RUPERT KNEW nothing of the King's escape when he
launched his forces across the Pennines from Preston on 23
June. Deep in the Yorkshire dales at Skipton, where the castle
was held by a small royalist garrison, he allowed himself three
days' halt, to see to it that all his hastily assembled regiments
were fully armed and ready for action. From there, two long
days' marches took him by way of Otley to Knaresborough,
where he quartered on the 30th a mere eighteen miles from his
objective. The generals before York had already decided they
must come out and fight before he reached it, even if it meant
raising the siege. This they hoped to avoid, for the Earl of
Denbigh and Sir John Meldrum were on their way with some
local forces from the midlands, and these should have sufficed
with a bit of reinforcement to keep the entrenchments manned
while the main armies went out to dispute Rupert's advance.
But Rupert's speed brought him within a day's march when
Denbigh and Meldrum were still four days distant, so Leven,
Manchester and Fairfax had to move out with all their men
to intercept him. It went hard with them to abandon their
lines, for they left behind them their siege pieces, ammunition
and (among other gear) four thousand new pairs of boots and
shoes to be joyfully plundered by the besieged. But no other
course was possible; York after all would be at their mercy if
they beat Rupert. They rather over-estimated his numerical
strength, but he was not a general to meet with inferior numbers if it could be helped, and their first aim must be to prevent him from adding Newcastle's defending forces to his own.

What they underestimated was his speed and skill in manœuvre. Choosing for their ground the wide expanse of heath
north-west of Long Marston, they thought they commanded
any feasible route he could take from Knaresborough to York,

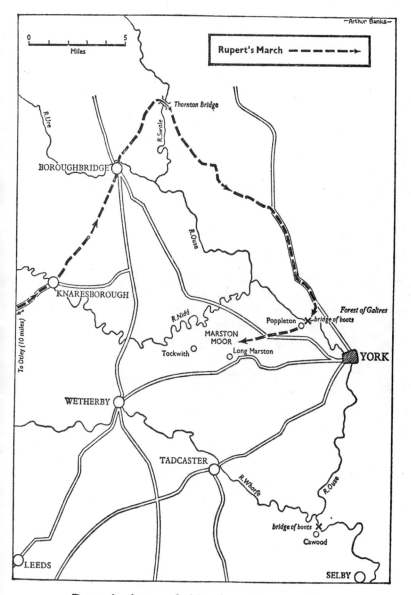

Rupert's Approach March to Marston Moor

for the Ouse bounded his passage to the north, and even if he crossed it at Boroughbridge, the first bridge above York, he would still have the Swale to negotiate. In any case Manchester had a bridge of boats over the Ouse at nearby Poppleton, guarded by a regiment of dragoons, so he was not cut off from the country north of the city in the unlikely event of Rupert's approaching it that way. But Rupert did what none of his opponents would have attempted in a single day. Striking rapidly north-east on 1 July, he crossed the Ouse at Boroughbridge and the Swale at Thornton Bridge, then marched down the left bank of the Ouse in time to capture the bridge of boats and open the way into York before a finger could be lifted to stop him. His infantry marched twenty-two miles that day before they quartered in the forest of Galtres, but the city was relieved. Some of his cavalry kept the roads which led into it, while other regiments passed over the bridge of boats and threw out a screen on Marston Moor, keeping the allied armies under observation. With these was Rupert himself, eager for battle next day and anxious to reconnoitre his enemies' position and the terrain on which he might fight them. He did not enter York himself that night, but sent in Goring with a message to Newcastle to have all his troops ready by four the next morning to march out and join him on the Moor. The Marquis had sent him a fulsome letter of congratulation, declaring that he was 'made of nothing but thankfulness and obedience to Your Highness's commands'. Rupert took these professions quite simply at their face value – his first serious mistake in a brilliantly executed piece of strategy.

There was little rest for his cavalry that night, and little comfort for his opponents. The three allied armies found what quarter they could in and around Long Marston, but lodging was scarce, and so was food. Even the wells were soon drained dry, and the soldiers had to drink what they could from puddles and ditches. Most of the cavalry slept out on the Moors, their horses' tethers in their hands.

Their general and field officers met for a council of war before they retired to rest. The English commanders were keener than the Scots to bring Rupert to battle at once, but it was not obvious how they could best make sure of doing so. There was certainly no indication yet that he would meet them on the ground they had chosen that day. Having just successfully evaded them, why should he come out and fight them tomorrow, when even with Newcastle's men he stood to be outnumbered by three to two? He had already raised the siege, and by striking elsewhere he might well reckon on drawing off enough of the besieging forces to prevent it from being effectively resumed. Might he not make another dash for Newark, and thence break into the rich, exposed territory of the Eastern Association? That would certainly suffice to draw off Manchester's army. Or, even more to be feared, he might be planning to join forces with the King somewhere in the midlands. That, with Essex far away in the west and Waller half-broken, was to be averted at all costs. Thus the three generals took stock of Rupert's probable intentions – plausibly enough, though they reckoned too little with his thirst for battle and his fear for the King's imagined danger, and they could not of course know of the letter Charles had written to him on 14 June. As they saw it, Rupert must be made to fight if possible, but he must not be given the slightest chance to slip through.

Accordingly they ordered an early march by their combined armies to Tadcaster, intending to push on at once to Cawood and Selby. By holding these crossings of the Wharfe and Ouse they would bar Rupert's route south. They had a bridge of boats at Cawood, and should he decide to remain in York it was doubly important to secure this, now that they had lost the similar bridge at Poppleton, if they were to dispute the territory east and south of the city with him.

And so on the morning of Tuesday, 2 July, the foot streamed off southward with the Scots in the van, while 3000 horse and dragoons stayed in the Marston area to cover their rear and watch for any movements by the enemy. They had not long to wait, for Rupert had been passing his forces over the Ouse at Poppleton since four in the morning, and parties of his cavalry were soon to be seen on the Moor. These at first sight gave no cause for alarm, for it was to be expected that he would watch his opponents as they watched him. When they saw one body of his horse which had faced them for a time wheel off the Moor out of sight, they took it as confirmation that he meant to break through southward.[1] But gradually more and more of his horsemen appeared, 5000 by about nine o'clock, and it became clear that these were no mere reconnaissance forces but the main body of his army. He might even attack while the parliamentary infantry was strung out for eight miles along the lanes to Tadcaster, with the baggage all vulnerable in its rear. At any rate it was Rupert who was evidently forcing an engagement, and the three generals (who had remained at Long Marston) were going to be lucky if they could get their men collected and formed up for battle before he fell on them. An urgent order went out to the foot to return, but it did not reach the Scots at the head of the column until they were within a mile or two of Tadcaster.

An anxious two or three hours ensued during which the horse, temporarily outnumbered, faced Rupert's forces as they deployed upon the Moor. But Rupert was having his own difficulties. Newcastle came out with a troop of gentlemen of quality to meet him at about nine, but of his infantry, which Rupert had expected to march from York four or five hours earlier, there was no sign. 'My Lord', said the Prince, 'I wish you had come sooner with your forces, but I hope we shall yet have a glorious day.' He had counted on immediate obedience to a peremptory command, without reckoning either the injury to the Marquis's pride at his unceremonious assumption of superior authority or the expectation of the northern infantry that after the long, gruelling siege they would be allowed some rest and reward. In fact, the foot *had* been drawn

1. Some writers, following Manchester's chaplain Simeon Ash, have interpreted this as a deliberate feint by Rupert which succeeded in drawing off his opponents to the south. But Watson's and Stockdale's narratives make it clear that the Tadcaster march had been decided upon the evening before, and it had probably begun before this incident occurred.

up in the city in the early hours of the morning, but it then transpired that large numbers of them had not returned from plundering the besiegers' lines. Those that did turn out, being due for pay, refused to march until they got it, and it was said that Lord Eythin, who frankly did not want to denude the garrison at Rupert's behest, did nothing to discourage their mutinous spirit. Had Robert known Newcastle better, he should not have been surprised when the Marquis urged all the reasons he could think of for avoiding immediate action, preferably for two or three days until Colonel Clavering arrived with a small royalist force from Cumberland and Westmorland. Rupert on the other hand was for attacking at once, even before Newcastle's foot came up; their absence, he thought, would not count so heavily as the disorder in which he would catch the rebels before their own infantry could be brought into the fight. Just how great a risk he would have run cannot be calculated at this distance of time; we do not know how much of the allied cavalry was in a position to engage him, or whether any of their foot was still within fighting distance. Rupert might conceivably have brought off another Newark, but the cost of failure would have been far heavier this time, and his enemies would never have allowed his reputation to survive it. At any rate, he was persuaded to wait for the foot.

At least he was strong enough on the ground during the morning to choose exactly where he would fight. His front faced southward, and stretched through a shallow concave arc nearly two miles long. His left flank lay just north of Long Marston, his right rested almost on Tockwith. Three features of the terrain need to be stressed, two of them not at all obvious to those who tramp the battlefield today, for the process of enclosure has wrought great changes in the scene. The first was the contrast between Marston Moor, stretching northward flat and featureless behind the royalist front, and Marston Field, rising opposite in broad enclosures, mostly under rye. It was in these rye-fields that the Scots and parliamentarians had to take up their positions. The Moor itself is all enclosed now, but it was then open ground in which cavalry could

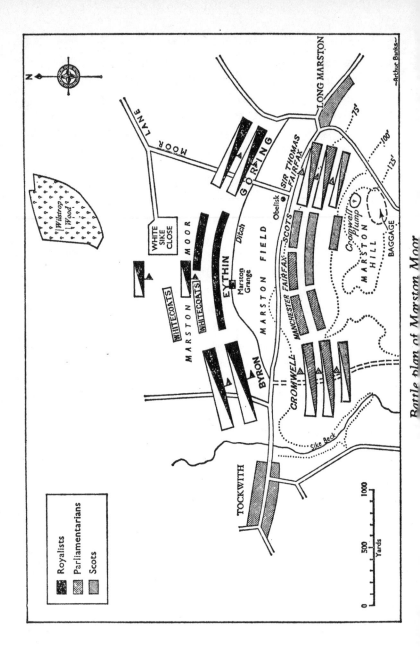

Battle plan of Marston Moor

operate freely, except at the eastern end where a profusion of furze bushes and ditches made the going more difficult. The second feature was the obstacle, a long ditch or drain, which divided the Moor from the fields. It was close behind this that Rupert stationed his cavalry, and such infantry as he had with him, to deny the Moor to his opponents. From about the centre eastwards, the ditch was apparently deep and lined by a hedge, but it was shallower and less formidable towards its western end, where it curved round to peter out near the junction of Kendal Lane with the Tockwith–Marston road.[1] Rupert lined this ditch with musketeers, choosing his own and Lord Byron's regiments of foot for the task. Such a screen was often thrown out before an army's main front; it was known as a 'forlorn hope', and its job was to harass and disrupt an enemy attack as far as it could before falling back on its main body. Posted as it was in this instance, it made the ditch a nasty obstacle to tackle – especially for the cavalry – before coming to grips with the main royalist forces close behind it. The third feature of the ground, more obvious today, was the slight ridge running east and west just below the Tockwith–Marston road, which gave the Scots and parliamentarians the advantage of a gentle downhill slope for their initial charge. It is only slight, for its highest point, the tree-crowned prominence near the western end still known as Cromwell's Plump, rises barely a hundred feet above the ditch and the Moor.

Lord Eythin eventually brought the infantry from York on to the Moor at some time between two and four in the afternoon, when the enemy foot, back from their vain trek to Tadcaster, were taking up their positions. Eythin when he met Rupert was incapable even of the courtesy with which New-

1. Most plans of the battle show the ditch running all the way in a roughly straight line, parallel with the Tockwith–Marston road. But the late eighteenth-century enclosure map of Tockwith (kept in the parish church) shows the western end of the ditch as I have indicated it in the plan, and a close inspection of the ground and of air photographs has convinced me that this irregularly curved line, still marked by a hedge and a drain, represents an older and more natural feature than the other field-boundaries in the area.

castle cloaked his most frustrating objections. He bore the
Prince a grudge which went back nearly six years to the obscure
action before Lemgo in Germany in which Rupert had been
captured, and in which Eythin, then plain James King, was
judged to have let him down badly. Rumour had even spoken
of treachery, and Eythin did not forgive the imputation. He
now objected to Rupert's placing of his forces because they
were too near the enemy, but when Rupert offered to draw
them back somewhat he testily answered 'No, sir, it is too late'.
And when Rupert explained with a sketch map how he meant
to fight the battle, Eythin's only response was 'By God, sir, it
is very fine in the paper, but there is no such thing in the field'.
Eythin, like Newcastle, was dead against fighting at all that
day. 'Sir', he taunted, 'your forwardness lost us the day in
Germany, where yourself was taken prisoner.' Was it to meet
such a spirit as this that Rupert had marched and fought from
Shrewsbury to York? Faced with Newcastle's courtly tepidity
and Eythin's carping inaction after yesterday's long strain and
the night's exertions, it was not strange if some of the fire went
out of him as he watched his best chances of victory tick away
hour by hour.

By four o'clock both sides had at last completed the elaborate
process of drawing up their forces in 'battalia', with the cavalry
(as was usual in an open field) on either flank and the infantry
in the centre. They faced each other at what to modern eyes
would seem suicidally close range – the extreme flanks indeed
within musket shot, which meant four hundred yards at the
most. Rupert placed his own horse, at least 2600 strong, on
his right wing, where he knew it would meet Cromwell's. His
Major-General of the horse, Sir John Hurry, a seasoned professional who had changed sides once and was to do so twice
again, drew it up for him after the Swedish fashion, in squadrons interspersed with groups of fifty musketeers, whose fire
would gall his opponents if they charged first. Lord Byron
commanded the first line, Lord Molyneux the second or reserve. The infantry of the centre, numbering about 11,000,
was ranged in three lines, the regiments which Rupert had

brought with him in the first under Colonel Tillier, Newcastle's (being late on the field) forming part of the second and
all of the third under Sir Francis Mackworth. These whitecoats
of Newcastle's – so called from the undyed woollen cloth from
which their jackets were cut – were soon to show that after
their mutinous behaviour in York they could still die like
heroes. Smaller bodies of cavalry were posted between the
second and third lines of foot and behind the third. The rear-
ward one included Rupert's life guard, and suggests the position from which he hoped to direct the battle. Lord Goring
commanded the left wing, consisting of the regiments with
which he had joined Rupert in Lancashire and totalling up-
wards of 2000 horse. Like the right wing it was drawn up in
two lines, with companies of musketeers supporting the squadrons of the first, and Sir Charles Lucas in command of the
second. Thus the royal armies numbered in all, including the
'forlorn', about 18,000 men.

The forces which Leven, as the senior allied general, marshalled in face of them were nearly half as many again, though
their superiority was almost all in infantry; the horse were more
nearly matched. The Scots furnished three-fifths of the allied
infantry but no more than 2000 mounted troops, and those
rode 'little light Scotch nags' which would make them less
than a match for the well-mounted gentlemen of Rupert's and
Goring's regiments in the charge. There were very slightly
more Scots than Englishmen on the allied front, but Manchester's 8000 men from the Eastern Association and the Fairfaxes'
5000 Yorkshire and Lancashire levies were much stronger
in cavalry. The allied front, which owing to the nature of the
ground was slightly shorter over-all than Rupert's, had its right
flank protected by hedges. The left was more open, but some
troops of Scottish dragoons – mounted infantry which were often used to secure such an outlying tactical feature as this–held
a 'cross ditch' close to Tockwith which was probably Sike Beck.
Earlier in the day Rupert had sent a party to try to gain the
mild rise south-east of Tockwith which the beck skirts, but
it had been beaten off, and it was on this ground that Cromwell

drew up the left wing of the allied cavalry. His first and second lines, together not far short of 2500 strong, consisted of his own fine troops from the Eastern Association, and for a third line he had three Scottish regiments, much under strength and numbering about 800 in all. But with them was David Leslie, who was to prove a pillar of strength to Cromwell in the battle. The great body of foot in the centre was grouped in brigades between 800 and 1500 strong, each consisting of at least two regiments. There were six brigades in the first line, two from each army: Manchester's on the left, closest to their cavalry, and commanded by Major-General Crawford; Lord Fairfax's in the centre; and Scotsmen on the right, led by Lieutenant-General William Baillie. The second line consisted all of Scots, except for a third brigade of Manchester's on the left, and farther back there was another Scottish brigade as reserve. The Scots, in fact, were given the positions they could take up most quickly, coming as they did last to the field after leading the march to Tadcaster. The right wing consisted of Sir Thomas Fairfax's cavalry, weaker than Cromwell's, but similarly drawn up and supported like his by about 800 Scottish horse.

The allied armies had about twenty-five guns ranged along their ridge, and Rupert placed a few of his right forward in the ditch. A desultory exchange of fire began at about two o'clock, enough to persuade Byron to move his cavalry back a little, though it caused very few casualties on either side. Close as the armies were, the distance was greater than the light field-pieces of those days could throw their little three-pound balls with any accuracy. By about five a quiet fell upon the two armies, and the royalists could hear their opponents chanting their metrical psalms in Marston Field. It was a comfort to taut nerves and tired muscles to sing the songs of an earlier chosen people, for these soldiers had to stand a test which modern warfare has forgotten – that of watching for hours, without cover and at a range close enough for every detail to be seen, a whole enemy army poised rank on rank for battle, arms glinting, colours flying, and all the panoply of death flaunting its gayest colours. These soldiers were hungry and thirsty too after their wild-goose chase that morning, and intermittent showers added to their discomfort as they stood amidst the tall, sodden rye. But as the long summer evening drew slowly on they began to wonder if they would fight at all that day.

Rupert, soon after seven, decided they would not. Rashly he assumed that his opponents would conclude as he did that it was too late in the day to bring on so great an engagement. 'We will charge them tomorrow morning', he told Newcastle. He retired to eat his supper, some distance away from his troops, many of whom lay down to snatch some rest. The Marquis withdrew to his coach to smoke a pipe. The sky darkened, and at half past seven great peals of thunder heralded a sudden hailstorm. Just as it broke, the whole allied line surged down the slope, and at once the din of battle rose high and sharp above the storm. The clashing armies, wrote a captain who fought with Cromwell, 'made such a noise with shot and clamour of shouts that we lost our ears, and the smoke of powder was so thick that we saw no light but what proceeded from the mouths of guns'. The ditch before Rupert's front was quickly crossed along the line. To Manchester's chaplain Simeon Ash, standing on Marston Hill, 'our army in its several parts, moving down the hill, was like unto so many thick clouds'. He watched Manchester's own brigades of foot pause after advancing two hundred paces for a brief exchange of fire with the 'forlorn hope' lining the ditch, then advance again to drive it back in disorder and capture four guns. Fairfax's foot and the Scots to the right also got across at first, though they were not long to maintain their ground. But the charge went best of all on the left, where the Scots dragoons quickly cleared the ditch for Cromwell's horse to cross in almost unbroken order – 'the bravest sight in the world', wrote Scoutmaster-General Watson, who was in the charge with Cromwell,

two such disciplined armies marching to a charge. We came down the hill in the bravest order, and with the greatest resolution that ever was seen. . . . In a moment we were past the ditch into the Moor, upon equal grounds with the enemy, our men going in a running march.

Byron did not wait to receive the charge standing, but advanced to meet it head on. It was a natural reaction, and generally a sound one; for the cavalry of that time charged in close order, almost knee to knee, and at a smart trot rather than a gallop, relying on the sheer weight of impact for their greatest effect. But Byron not only masked the fire of the musketeers posted between his squadrons, he landed himself at the moment of collision in a piece of marshy ground which should have served for his surer defence and the confusion of his attackers. His whole first line was quickly routed, and probably part of the second too.

Rupert, roused by the firing and the shouting, rode at once towards his disordered right wing with such troops from his reserve and his life guard as he could collect at a moment's notice. Soon he met the men of his own regiment in flight. "Swounds, do you run?' he shouted; 'follow me.' He rallied them and the yet unbroken squadrons for a sharp and protracted struggle. Watson describes it from the other side:

> Cromwell's own division had a hard pull of it, for they were charged by Rupert's bravest men both in front and flank. They stood at the sword's point a pretty while, hacking one another; but at last (it so pleased God) he broke through them, scattering them before him like a little dust. At the same instant the rest of our horse of that wing had wholly broken all Prince Rupert's horse on their right wing, and were in chase of them beyond their left wing.

Just how serious a check Cromwell's horse received from Rupert's counter-charge is a matter on which contemporary witnesses disagree. The strain and excitement of battle play odd tricks with one's sense of time, and the confusion was such that it was natural enough for impressions to differ, even when they were not coloured by the bitter partisanship which soon developed around the figure of Cromwell. What seems to have happened is that his first line was temporarily repulsed and somewhat disordered, but that Leslie charged the royalist horse in the flank, enabling the Ironsides to recover their advantage and complete the rout. Of the outcome there is no doubt; Rupert's whole right wing was soon 'flying along by Wilstrop Wood as fast and as thick as could be', and nothing more could be done to rally it. At this point the discipline and battle-sense of Cromwell's cavalry stood out in a manner which was destined to decide the day. The victorious regiments were not allowed to spread out in headlong pursuit over the fields and lanes towards York, as every instinct would urge them to do with a beaten enemy flying before them, but were halted on the field and re-formed. It was as well, for there was work for them still to do.

Whether Cromwell personally made this vital check is doubt-ful. Early in the action he was slightly wounded in the neck, and quite probably, though the story only comes from sources hostile to him, he left the field for a brief while to have his wound dressed, leaving Leslie to command in his absence.[1] But there is no doubt that he was back with Leslie in the second great cavalry action which clinched the victory, an action which will fall into place when we have turned to other parts of the field.

Immediately to the right of Cromwell's horse, Manchester's foot under Crawford fought with similar success, rapidly driving back the westernmost regiments of Rupert's foot. In-deed the whole allied left routed or folded up the royalist right in less than an hour, wheeling to the right as it did so until

1. Until an aircraft crashed on it in the last war, a cottage stood at the eastern end of Tockwith which was pointed out as the place where Cromwell's wound was dressed. If the tradition can be trusted, Cromwell would have had only about 400 yards to ride to it from where he first engaged Byron's horse. Colonel Marcus Trevor, who commanded a regiment in Byron's front line, claimed to have in-flicted the wound with his own sword (Brit. Mus., Harleian MSS. 4180, fol. 142) – which is likelier than the story in other sources that Cromwell was hurt by the accidental discharge of one of his own troopers' pistols.

the cavalry on its left flank was facing roughly eastward. Had the same success attended Fairfax's horse, the royalist infantry would soon have been enveloped. But without Cromwell or Leslie yet knowing it their comrades on the right had come close to disaster. Sir Thomas Fairfax had found the ditch and its hedge a much more formidable obstacle than it proved on Cromwell's front, and beyond it the ground was so broken with clumps of furze and minor ditches that his cavalry was at a heavy disadvantage. He managed to get about four hundred of his own men across, but before he could wait and re-form his front line as a whole the fire of the musketeers posted between Goring's squadrons proved so harassing that he was forced to charge at once. A severe spell of hand-to-hand fighting ensued, which ended with that particular section of Goring's front which he engaged breaking and flying. But his casualties were severe; scarcely an officer who charged with him came through unscathed. He himself was cut in the cheek, and a shot struck his horse. His brother Charles was mortally wounded, and so was Lambert's major, another Fairfax, whose body bore no less than thirty wounds. The troops which broke through pursued the royalists they had beaten towards York, but it was only a part of Goring's front line that had been broken, and when Sir Thomas turned back (as he soon did) to direct the rest of his wing he found himself alone among squadrons of enemy horse.

The royalist cavalry, all but that part which he had engaged, had charged his wavering second line, consisting largely of raw levies, and had put it to flight. Only the Scottish horse in the rear, notably Lord Eglinton's regiment, attempted to stand their ground, but they were too few to stem the onrush. Some of Goring's squadrons charged right through to the top of Marston Hill and beyond, to plunder the baggage train and pursue the fugitives far off the field. To make matters worse a considerable body of spectators, who had come to the hill for a grandstand view of the battle, took to their heels in confusion, and the panic spread to the reserve of Scottish infantry posted nearby. The second line of Goring's cavalry followed up the advantage and launched successive charges against the right flank of the allied foot as it stood locked in battle with Rupert's infantry. They also wrought havoc among the Scots of the second line, who were already disordered, and some of them even trampled down, by the flight of the cavalry on their right. In the centre Lord Fairfax's brigades of foot, fighting beyond the ditch, broke before a furious onslaught by Newcastle's whitecoats, and many of the Scots on their right were also put to flight. A gentleman who reached the battlefield at this stage with a message for Rupert from Ormond found all in chaos:

> in the fire, smoke and confusion of that day [he wrote] I knew not for my soul whither to incline. The runaways on both sides were so many, so breathless, so speechless, so full of fears, that I should not have taken them for men, but by their motion, which still served them very well; both armies being mingled, both horse and foot, no side keeping their own posts.

He records vivid glimpses of a shoal of Scots fleeing past him crying, 'wae's us, we are all undone', of a ragged troop of horse reduced to four men and a cornet, and of 'a little foot officer without hat, band, sword or indeed anything but feet and so much tongue as would serve to enquire the way to the next garrisons'.

Leven himself was caught in the flood of fugitives, and after making a vain attempt to rally them he fled too, believing the battle lost. So did Lord Fairfax, his men having broken, and all along the roads to the south ran news of a royalist victory. Even Manchester seems to have been on the point of flight, though chaplain Ash says that he eventually rallied about five hundred men and brought them back to the field. As a Scottish chaplain who was there quaintly put it, 'God would not have a general in the army; He himself was general'.

But all was not yet lost on that shattered right wing of the allied armies. Two very gallant Scottish regiments, the Earl of Lindsay's and Lord Maitland's, which being on the very right of the first line of foot were particularly exposed, stuck grimly to their ground. When they had stood up to two cavalry charges, Lieutenant-General Baillie and Major-General Lumsden managed to bring to their support some more regiments which had resisted the rout of the second line. In this action the pike came into its own, for only by the pikemen kneeling with butts of their sixteen-foot-long staves stuck in the ground could these Scots withstand the simultaneous assaults of both horse and foot. Even so a third charge shook them severely. But they not only weathered it, they took Sir Charles Lucas prisoner. They even made ground against the royalist foot. How much longer they could have held out unaided one cannot tell, but help was on the way. Whereas so far the two halves of the battle, the allied success on one wing and the royalist on the other, had each developed in ignorance of the other's fate, events now brought the victors of both into decisive collision.

We left Sir Thomas Fairfax wounded and isolated among strong bodies of royalist cavalry. He promptly did the only thing that would save him from immediate capture. As a means of recognition in the confusion of the battle, his side was wearing as a 'field sign' white bands or papers in their hats, for although the men of some regiments wore coats of a single colour there was nothing approaching uniform among their commanders. Sir Thomas took the band from his hat, passed through his opponents as one of themselves, and made his way to Cromwell's victorious cavalry, now probably halted and facing east behind where the whitecoats were fighting. Whether he or other remnants of his command informed them of the disaster on the right, or whether the news had passed along from the exposed right flank of Crawford's foot, Cromwell and Leslie led their regiments round between Wilstrop Wood and the rear of the battle to challenge Goring's horse on the very ground where it had first fought. Crawford's infantry brigades still marched and fought on their right. Now, however, the directions were reversed. Goring's troops, who had believed victory to be theirs already, had to face north to meet a charge from the Moor. They were not up against raw troops now, and this time they broke and fled; this time, too, Cromwell could spare some squadrons to pursue them towards York.

But though the brave Scots were now relieved, one more task awaited Cromwell's and Leslie's weary troopers. They were needed to break a last desperate resistance by Newcastle's whitecoats, who had already done so much to reverse the early success of the allied foot and were now prepared to spend their last gasp to save the long defence of York from being wasted. Penned in White Sike Close, and attacked in flank and rear by Cromwell's and Leslie's cavalry, it was well said of their white coats that they had 'brought their winding-sheets about them into the field'. For long neither horse nor foot could break their ranks; so solid did their pikemen stand that dragoons were called in to force a gap for cavalry to enter. Even when their square was thus broken they fought on, those who were too badly wounded to stand struggling with their swords or pikes to gore the bellies of the horses who rode over them. It was rare in the Civil War for men in their plight to refuse quarter, but these men did, and their valour moved Cromwell's troopers to pity. They died in ranks as they fought, and barely thirty were taken alive.

It was almost dark when the slaughter was over; the whole battle had lasted about two hours – less rather than more. But a bright moon helped Cromwell's victorious cavalry to pursue the royalist horse most of the way to York, and for three miles a line of slain and wounded marked the path of their swords. Rupert only narrowly escaped capture – his enemies said by hiding in a beanfield – before he returned to the city at about eleven o'clock. There his officers 'came dropping in one by one, not knowing, but marvelling and doubting, what fortune might befall one another'. It was a pitiful sight within the walls, with the whole of Micklegate from the Bar onwards crammed with wounded, stretched in the streets and crying out in their agony.

The victors all returned at length to the field, where they sang their psalm of victory and camped down for the night. Most of them slept hungry; food was still very short, and for a second night they had only the ditches and puddles to quench their thirst. Their wagons had thrice been plundered during the day – by Goring's troopers, by their own runaways and by a riff-raff of hangers-on who followed the army for what they could pick up. Manchester rode round his regiments of horse and foot at about eleven that night, thanking them and urging them to give the honour of victory to God alone – promising also to provide for them better in the morning than he could that night. He was the only one of the three generals present. Lord Fairfax was at Cawood, and no one quite knew whether Leven was at Wetherby or Leeds or Bradford; neither returned until Thursday. Meanwhile their troops exercised their gruesome privilege of stripping the enemy dead, who were to be seen next morning lying naked in their thousands, a few still stirring with the wretched remnants of life. Sir Charles Lucas, who was taken round them so that he might pick out whom he would for a better burial than the common pits, could not but weep for the multitude of them, exclaiming 'Alas for King Charles! Unhappy King Charles!' Recognizing a bracelet woven of hair about one poor corpse's wrist, he asked that it might be taken off, saying that 'an honourable lady would give thanks for it'. The countrymen who had the burying of the royalist dead numbered them at 4150. The victorious armies, on the other hand, lost no more than 300 killed, though many more were wounded. They had 1500 prisoners on their hands, including three of major-general's rank and a son of Goring's, and they had taken besides about 6000 arms, all the royalist ordnance, powder and baggage, and about a hundred colours. Not all the latter reached London, for though the captor of a standard could claim a reward of ten shillings, the soldiers loved to cut them into pieces to wear as trophies.

One further encounter needs to be recorded, a painful meeting some time in the night or early morning after the battle between Rupert and Newcastle and Eythin. Newcastle had fought as best he could at the head of a troop of gentlemen volunteers, but he had no more influenced the course of the battle than any cornet of horse. Rupert, whose sole thought was of how best and soonest to recover from their defeat, was shocked to find both Newcastle and Eythin determined to quit the country. He urged the Marquis to recruit his shattered forces so that they might fight again. 'No,' replied Newcastle, 'I will not endure the laughter of the court.' Had he forgotten a letter the King had written him with his own hand less than three months ago? 'The truth is,' Charles had said, 'if either you or my Lord Eythin leave my service I am sure at least all the north (I speak not all I think) is lost. Remember, all courage is not in fighting; constancy in a good cause being the chief, and the despising of slanderous tongues not the least, ingredient.'

Rupert rode out of York on the Wednesday morning with what troops he could salve from the wreckage – no more than 6000 at the start, though he picked up Clavering's forces on his first day's march, and paused at Richmond to collect more stragglers from the battle. There too Montrose came to him – a strange meeting between two young soldiers, the one bent on a crazy adventure that was soon to make a legend of him, the other fiercely casting off the temptation to despair over his shattering defeat. Montrose had come in the hope of borrowing just a thousand horse wherewith to cut his way into the heart of Scotland. But Rupert could spare none; swiftly he led what was left of his army back over the Pennines into Lancashire, and thence to Chester. But there was no pursuit. Even had they not been too short of provisions to attempt it, one doubts whether any of the three victorious generals would have thought any further than the capture of York.

That was soon effected. After two days the allied armies returned to their lines before the city, where Sir Thomas Glemham, left in charge of the hopelessly depleted garrison, had no choice but to negotiate a surrender. He consented to terms on 16 July which were generous in the circumstances. His men were to march out with the honours of war – arms shouldered, colours flying, the musketeers with bullets between their teeth and match lit at both ends – with an escort to take them to the nearest royalist garrison at Skipton. The new garrison of York was to consist of at least two-thirds of Yorkshiremen, with Lord Fairfax as Governor. A precious clause guaranteed all churches and other buildings from defacement; it may have saved the glory of the Minster's glass for posterity.

The war in the north was decided. Towns like Newcastle and Carlisle, castles like Pontefract and Scarborough, might prolong resistance to the end, but there was no hope for them now unless a new army could be raised for the King north of Trent. It never was, on a scale that could count; something of the heart went out of the King's cause in the north parts after Newcastle sailed for Holland. Whether the Parliament and the Scots could use their victory to bring the whole war to a successful conclusion was, however, a different matter.

Rupert hides after the Battle in a bean-field near York, whilst his pet dog Boy lies dead on the field. Soldiers capture his baggage horses and discover documents and crucifixes in his 'private cabinet'

From a satirical pamphlet

4

Winter of Discontent

IF THE VICTORS of Marston Moor had known how to seize their chances, they could have won the war by the end of the year. Purely local forces apart, Charles had about 10,000 men with him in the field, Maurice less than half as many before Lyme and Rupert the cavalry he had salvaged from his defeat – that was almost all. Against these might have been concentrated the Scots and the armies of Essex, Manchester and Waller, for the north and midlands could now be left to the strong local forces of the Fairfaxes, Brereton, Denbigh and Meldrum. Why were all the chances missed? It was partly sheer folly; partly, too, that the will to seize them was as lacking for a time as the skill.

The most calamitous folly was Essex's, in persisting in his mad march into the west. Much as gallant little Lyme and its Governor Robert Blake deserved relief, Parliament's main army in the south had bigger work to do. Essex was still thinking only of recovering territory, at a stage when the war was to be decided by pitched battles. Worse still, he left himself highly vulnerable. On 12 July Charles set off from Evesham in pursuit of him with an army at least equal to his own. Essex relieved Lyme, but by the time he got to Tavistock, Charles was already in Exeter and about to join forces with Maurice. Instead of sheltering behind Plymouth's defences till help could reach him, Essex took the crazy decision to plunge forward into Cornwall, calling loudly on Waller to make a diversion in his pursuers' rear. But trained band trouble had reduced Waller to barely 4000 men, and all he could send were 2000 horse under Lieutenant-General Middleton. Essex found the Cornishmen hostile to a man, and Hopton's and Sir Richard Grenville's local forces brought the King's strength up to 16,000. Essex had about 10,000 when he reached Lostwithiel, and that was as far as he got. All through August the royalists tightened the net round the hungry, dispirited parliamentarians. Their operations were both skilful and determined, Essex's feeble and supine. On the 31st, with surrender staring him in the face, Essex sent off his cavalry to cut their way out and escape to Plymouth. The rest of that day his infantry fought their retreat down the Fowey estuary till they would fight no more. Essex slipped away by sea early next morning, leaving Major-General Skippon to bear the humiliation of surrender. Nearly 6000 men had to hand over their arms, including about forty guns, though they themselves were allowed to march away on condition they did not fight again until they had reached Southampton or Portsmouth. It was the most resounding royalist victory of the war.

Meanwhile the three generals who had beaten Rupert and taken York commended to Parliament 'the procuring of a settled peace unto the kingdoms' and took a long rest on their laurels. The Scots quartered about Leeds and Wakefield until five weeks after the battle, when Leven at last led them off to resume the siege of Newcastle. Lord Fairfax garrisoned York and prepared unhurriedly to reduce the remaining royalist strongholds in the country. Manchester, after a short stay at Doncaster, returned to Lincoln early in August and stuck there for a whole month. His officers begged him to let them march against Newark, and the Committee of Both Kingdoms pressed him to send help to Brereton against Rupert, who was busy recruiting again. He put off these repeated appeals with every kind of evasion; in the seven weeks after the fall of York he called only one council of war. That his forces did reduce two or three minor royal garrisons was due only to the pressure of his own subordinates. One of these was Lieutenant-Colonel John Lilburne, who commanded his dragoons; he heard that Tickhill Castle was only waiting for a decent excuse to surrender, and asked leave to march against it. 'Get thee gone!' cried Manchester angrily, 'thou art a mad fellow.' Lilburne took this for permission, captured Tickhill without firing a shot, and returned to be furiously rated by his general before his own prisoners.

The disaster to Essex soon caused more urgent calls to be made on Manchester. During August Waller, who had occupied Abingdon, was sent westward with such poor forces as he could muster, and on the 22nd Manchester was ordered to the Oxford area to fill the gap. He lingered more than a fortnight at Lincoln before complying, and then led his army by such a long, slow detour through the Eastern Association that by 27 September he was still only at Harefield in Middlesex. Long before this, Parliament had become alarmed lest the victorious royalists should march against London, though in fact Charles was aiming no further for the moment than relieving his besieged garrisons in Basing House, Donnington Castle and Banbury. Fortunately too for Parliament he had wasted time on an ineffectual attempt against Plymouth before advancing eastward. But much still depended on Manchester obeying the urgent orders which he was now given. He was to send his cavalry ahead to Shaftesbury, where Waller's and Essex's horse were already concentrated, and march with his foot to Newbury to join Essex's infantry, which was now re-armed. Had he complied, Waller and Cromwell were convinced that the King could have been halted west of Salisbury. But Manchester sat tight at Reading until mid-October while the royalists entered Salisbury, forced Waller back through Andover and drove Donnington's besiegers into retreat.

Manchester, pricked into action at last, joined Waller at Basingstoke; and when Essex's foot and a brigade of London trained bands arrived to swell their infantry, they had the King at a disadvantage for the first time since June. With about 18,000 men they outnumbered him by a clear two to one, for many of his Cornishmen had gone home and he had sent off a brigade of cavalry to relieve Banbury. Charles turned northward and took up a defensive position at Newbury. His opponents had a chance of a victory that might have ruined him, and they bungled it miserably. They were, it is true, hampered by the Committee of Both Kingdoms trying too hard to direct the campaign from Westminster, and by Essex being ill at Reading. In the second battle of Newbury on 27 October they adopted a risky plan to storm the King's position simultaneously from east and west. The westward attack, despite a long approach march, achieved considerable success, but Manchester on the eastern side let it down badly. Despite the pleas of his officers, he refused to throw in his forces until well over an hour after the signal had been given for their assault. When at last he gave the order, the sun had already set and the whole operation failed. Darkness and sheer negligence enabled the royal army to escape almost intact to Oxford, and Manchester was justly blamed for preventing any effective pursuit. The parliamentarians were still at Newbury when Charles, reinforced now by Rupert, returned to nearby Donnington on 9 November to retrieve the guns he had had to leave behind. Twice he offered battle again, and twice the challenge was refused. The armies which had been so tardily concentrated against him were indeed no longer fit to fight, for hunger, sickness and demoralization had combined with the vile weather of that autumn to take the heart out of them. When they were ordered into the field to save Basing House from being relieved, so many ran away to Reading that the rest had to retreat there, leaving the siege to be abandoned.

Back at Oxford, Charles could feel he had gone far to redeem his defeat in the north. When a deputation of parliament men and Scots brought him fresh propositions for a peace treaty, he received them with something like derision. His only bad news lately had continued to come from the north, where the Scots had at last taken Newcastle, David Leslie was besieging Carlisle, Meldrum had recovered Liverpool and Helmsley had fallen to Lord Fairfax. But he had taken steps which he hoped would unify and strengthen authority in his armies for next year's campaigns. The Lords Wilmot and Percy, those trouble-making enemies of Rupert's, had been removed from their commands of the horse and the ordnance during the Lostwithiel campaign, to be replaced by Goring and Hopton. And now Charles at last made Rupert commander-in-chief of all his forces in place of old Brentford, though to avoid jealousies Rupert at his own request took the style of lieutenant-general under the nominal generalship of Prince Charles.

While Charles was taking pains to silence the quarrels among his own generals, he was much encouraged by the growing strife among those on the other side. When Leven, Manchester and Fairfax, after capturing York, urged Parliament to settle church government and renew its efforts for peace, they were really afraid of two things. One was that the Presbyterian religion which they hoped to see established in England was in danger from the more extreme and apocalyptic varieties of Puritanism which were spreading in the English forces, especially among Cromwell's cavalry, and in the City of London. If simple soldiers and citizens were to claim liberty of conscience for whatever heretical notions came into their heads, what would happen to the purity of the gospel – or to the invisible chains of authority that held the various degrees of men in their appointed places? The other fear was of the growing radicalism of the war-party leaders at Westminster, whose aims seemed now to go beyond the Covenant and at times to threaten monarchy itself. Both these fears came to focus on Cromwell, whom the Scots already looked upon as the most dangerous man in England. Manchester's army became a storm-centre during the autumn, rent between the factions of Cromwell, the commander of the horse, and Crawford, the narrow Presbyterian Scot who led the foot. Manchester himself, who had formerly leaned heavily on Cromwell, became wholly estranged from him.

The divisions among the officers reflected those at Westminster. The broad split between peace party and war party remained, and now questions of religion were deepening it. Already the great debate was on as to what forms of church government and worship should replace the old Anglican order. Most members of both Houses inclined to favour a single national church on Presbyterian lines, as the Solemn League and Covenant had promised. This appealed even to the many who were not particularly convinced of the divine right of

Presbytery, for it met their desire for a sober, uniform church discipline under the ultimate control of Parliament. But against the Presbyterians stood the Independents, who asked for liberty of conscience for all Protestant Christians and the right to associate for worship in their own way. This is not the place to go into the differences over church government between the Independents (the direct forebears of modern Congregationalists) and the Presbyterians. What matters is that the Independents asked for toleration not only for themselves but for the growing number of sects – Baptists, Seekers and scores of others – that were proliferating to the left of them. Independents and sectaries were among the most ardent supporters of the war and tended to be radical in politics; while radical politicians who were not religious enthusiasts – and a fair number were not – voted nevertheless with the Independents because of their alliance with the army. Liberty of conscience had no more ardent champions than Cromwell and his terrible cavalry. In this way 'Presbyterian' and 'Independent' became general terms for the right-wingers or peace party on the one hand and the left-wingers or war party on the other. For liberty of conscience was a social as well as a religious issue. The Presbyterian minister, who would probably owe his living and much of his authority in the parish to a gentleman of solid estate, could be a valuable social cement; the sectarian tub-preacher was social dynamite.

Manchester was a typical Presbyterian in this broad sense. He was neither a traitor nor a coward, nor yet the sort of man to stoop to merely personal jealousies. His integrity and magnanimity impressed even his opponents, and Clarendon was not the only royalist to praise his 'gentle and generous nature'. His conduct from Marston Moor to Newbury needs explaining. Historians have attributed his sudden distaste for fighting the King to a story that Vane, when he visited the camp before York in June, sounded the three generals there about the possibility of deposing Charles. But it is an unlikely story, resting only on the gossip picked up by foreign ambassadors. Manchester's whole attitude changed simply because Marston Moor transformed the character of the war. Before the battle, moderates like Manchester could feel they were fighting to save the parliamentary cause from total defeat; Marston Moor for the first time opened up the prospect of total victory. But it was just this prospect which appalled Manchester, once he began to face it. During those painful autumn months when his officers felt shamed by his inaction and his contempt for Parliament's orders, he often expressed himself freely. 'This war would not be ended by the sword', he would say, 'for if it were so concluded it would be an occasion of rising again or of a future quarrel. It would be better for the kingdom if it were ended by an accommodation.' God, he declared, had shown His will by making none of Parliament's victories decisive – and here divine providence was certainly getting every co-operation from Manchester. His frankest moment was at the council of war on 10 November, when the King's army was allowed to get away from Donnington without fighting. 'Gentlemen', he said in words that were vividly remembered:

> I beseech you let's consider what we do. The King cares not how oft he fights, but it concerns us to be wary, for in fighting we venture all to nothing. If we fight him a hundred times and beat him ninety-nine, we shall be hanged – we shall lose our estates, and our posterities be undone.

Cromwell however knew that having taken up the sword they could end the war no other way. Manchester might be right that victory would only bring further conflict in its train, but this was not so certain as that Charles, beaten or unbeaten, would never concede the essential points for which Parliament had gone to war. A peace on any terms that Charles would accept would be tantamount to surrender.

The Presbyterians detested Cromwell's growing influence on three main grounds. In the first place he was a leader of the war party, both in army and Parliament, and had become Manchester's severest critic. Another accusation was that he was promoting Independents and sectaries in his cavalry regiments so as to build up a powerful military party for himself and undermine the authority of Presbyterians like Crawford. Thirdly, by commissioning men of modest birth he was felt to be betraying the interests of his class.

It is true that ever since Cromwell had seen the heart of Essex's levies fail them in the first campaigns he had deliberately enlisted men to whom the war was a crusade. 'Your troopers', he had then told Hampden,

> are most of them old decayed serving men and tapsters, and such kind of fellows, and their troopers are gentlemen's sons, younger sons, persons of quality. Do you think that the spirits of such base and mean fellows will ever be able to encounter gentlemen that have honour, courage and resolution in them? You must get men of a spirit that is like to go as far as a gentleman will go, or else I am sure you will be beaten still.

If such a spirit mattered so much among mere troopers, how much more must it count in their officers! When the Suffolk committee objected that one of his troop commanders was not a gentleman, Cromwell replied,

> If you choose godly honest men to be captains of horse, honest men will follow them, and they will be careful to mount such. . . . I had rather have a plain russet-coated captain that knows what he fights for, and loves what he knows, than that which you call a gentleman and is nothing else. I honour a gentleman that is so indeed.

Cromwell was of the gentry himself, and never forgot it. 'It had been well', he wrote a little later, 'that men of honour and birth had entered into these employments, but why do they not appear? . . . Better plain men than none.'

In Puritan East Anglia, it was especially among the Independents and sectaries that Cromwell found the spirit he was looking for. 'If you look upon his own regiment of horse,' complained a Presbyterian officer, 'see what a swarm there is of those that call themselves the godly; some of them profess they have seen visions and had revelations.' The Scots commis-

sioners viewed with alarm and disgust the rise of 'these wild
and enormous people' and of Cromwell, 'that darling of the
sectaries', who promoted them. Cromwell returned the Scots'
distrust, for liberty of conscience had become an end in itself
to him, and he was accused of uttering an unguarded threat
to draw his sword against them if they tried to force their own
narrow ecclesiastical discipline on England. According to Manchester, he admitted wanting to fill the army with Independents, because they would resist a peace that 'might not stand
with those ends that honest men should aim at'. And other
loose words were brought up against him, to the effect that 'he
hoped to live to see never a nobleman in England', and that
'God would have no lording over His people'. Yet Cromwell
was no social revolutionary; a few years hence he would be
throwing all his weight against would-be levellers in order to
preserve what he called 'the ranks and orders of men, whereby
England hath been known for hundreds of years – a nobleman,
a gentleman, a yeoman'. His care for 'the people of God' and
his frustration with peace-party peers were carrying him into
indiscretions.

The climax came on 25 November when Waller and Cromwell brought their complaints against Manchester before the
House of Commons. Waller dwelt on the last humiliating
weeks of the Newbury campaign; Cromwell dealt in detail with
Manchester's 'backwardness to all action' ever since the capture
of York. The Commons set up a committee to examine the
charges, which were corroborated to the hilt by a distinguished
group of officers. Manchester's counter-charges in the Lords
explained his exasperation with Cromwell, but not his own
military record over the last four months. It was a bad business, this quarrel which set Scots against English, Lords against
Commons and officers against their generals; yet how else but
by bringing it to the highest tribunal could Cromwell prevent
the next year's campaign from being botched as the last had
been? The Scots saw it as 'a high and mighty plot of the
Independent party to have gotten an army for themselves under
Cromwell, with the ruin and shamefully unjust crushing of

Manchester's person; of dissolving the union of the nations, of abolishing the House of Lords, of dividing the House of Commons, . . . of setting up themselves on the ruins of all'. They hoped Cromwell had given them a chance to remove him from both army and Parliament, and they plotted with Essex and the peace-party leaders to impeach him as an 'incendiary' between the two kingdoms.

No one was more bewildered than the Scots when within a week the whole quarrel was dropped, and in a manner which promised to transform the conduct of the war.

A crowded House heard the report of the committee on the charges against Manchester on 9 December. As soon as it was read, Cromwell rose.

It is now time to speak [he said] or forever hold the tongue. The important occasion now is no less than to save a nation out of a bleeding, nay almost dying condition, which the long continuance of this war hath already brought it into. . . .

For what do the enemy say? Nay, what do many say that were friends at the beginning of the Parliament? Even this, that the members of both Houses have got great places and commands, and the sword into their hands; and what by interest in the Parliament, what by power into the army, will perpetually continue themselves in grandeur, and not permit the war speedily to end, lest their own power should determine with it. This that I speak here to our own faces, is but what others do utter abroad behind our backs. I am far from reflecting on any. I know the worth of those commanders, members of both Houses, who are yet in power; but . . . I do conceive that if the army be not put into another method, and the war more vigorously prosecuted, the people can bear the war no longer, and will enforce you to a dishonourable peace.

But this I would recommend to your prudence, not to insist upon any complaint or oversight of any commander-in-chief upon any occasion whatsoever; for as I must acknowledge myself guilty of oversights, so I know they can rarely be avoided in military matters. Therefore waiving a strict inquiry into the case of these things, let us apply ourselves to the remedy.

The remedy so plainly hinted by Cromwell was promptly moved by the chairman of the committee, a Presbyterian, and eagerly seconded by Vane, the leader of the Independents. It was that no member of either House should hold any command or office, military or civil, while the war lasted. Within an hour the Commons voted for an ordinance to be drafted on these lines – the first Self-Denying Ordinance – and ten days later they passed it.

Cromwell's plea for dropping all personal charges came the better because Manchester had conducted his side of the quarrel with decency and restraint, far above the muck-raking in which some other Presbyterian officers indulged. Cromwell for his part was offering to sacrifice his own military career as well as Manchester's. This original ordinance left no loophole whereby Cromwell could keep his command while Essex and Manchester lost theirs, unless both Houses chose to make a special exception of him. And when on 18 December the Commons expressly refused to exempt Essex from it, the Lords were hardly likely to do as much for Cromwell. Had the Lords passed the ordinance in its original form, Cromwell must have resigned his commission as Waller and many another member did. He refused to regard himself as indispensable. 'They do not idolize me', he said of his men, 'but look upon the cause they fight for.' But the Lords did not pass the ordinance; after shelving it for nearly three weeks they threw it out.

Meanwhile a still more important measure had come before the Commons, containing the positive part of Cromwell's plan for victory. It was a scheme, drafted by the Committee of Both Kingdoms, for throwing the existing field armies – Essex's, Waller's and Manchester's – into the melting-pot, and forging a new army out of their remains. Cromwell and Vane were the prime movers in this, and their objects were threefold. In the first place they wanted an army fit to fight wherever it was needed, unhampered by local ties or by trained bands, looking homeward over their shoulders. It was to be paid and supplied, not by local committees which might hold back when they thought their own defence was being neglected, but under Parliament's immediate authority. Secondly, its officers were to be full-time soldiers, not politicians or great magnates, and above all not peace-party men. And finally it was to enable Parliament to win the war without owing too much to the Scots. National pride played its part here, but stronger was the Independents' fear of a rigid, intolerant Presbyterianism, and stronger still their desire to be free of Scottish pressure when they eventually settled terms with the King.

Cromwell and Vane were the tellers when the Commons named the commander-in-chief of their New Model army. Their choice fell on Sir Thomas Fairfax. It was a bold one, for he was only thirty-two and had never commanded a full-scale army. He had not been lucky at Adwalton Moor and Marston Moor. But in the early West Riding campaigns, and above all at Winceby and Nantwich, he had shown besides conspicuous personal valour a swiftness and dash in exploiting daring opportunities that set him worlds apart from such as Essex and Manchester. With no political or religious axes to grind beyond a simple, selfless devotion to the cause he served, he was acceptable to Presbyterian and Independent alike. He was the sort of mild, even diffident man whom the fires of battle kindled to a white heat which communicated itself to all about him. His men loved him.

Under Fairfax, Skippon was an obvious choice as Major-General of the infantry. The post of Lieutenant-General, carrying the command of the horse, was left open, for if the Lords insisted on blocking the Self-Denying Ordinance they could hardly expect the Independents to exclude in advance so strong a claimant as Cromwell. And the question at the end of January 1645 was whether the Lords would pass the New Model Ordinance at all.

They delayed doing so while yet another peace negotiation was carried on with the King, this time at Uxbridge. The Scots were mainly responsible for it, and it foundered on the old rocks of episcopacy and the control of the armed forces. Charles's firmness on these points weakened the peace party sufficiently to get the New Model past the Lords, though only after a long tussle over the lists of officers and the commander-in-chief's powers to select and promote them. This surrender by the Lords was followed a few weeks later by another. On 3 April they passed a new Self-Denying Ordinance which the Commons had sent up to them, whereby peers and MPs must give up their offices and commands within forty days, but were not debarred from being reappointed. Essex and Manchester made it easier for them by resigning their commissions the day before.

It was time to be forging a new army, for the old ones were falling apart. The royalists, with the initiative very much in their hands, probed their weaknesses widely through the winter. Goring led a large-scale cavalry raid eastward through Hampshire and captured Farnham before he was forced to lead his exhausted, unpaid troopers back to Salisbury, pillaging and destroying indiscriminately as they went. Plymouth and Abingdon withstood strong assaults, but Weymouth was actually lost for three weeks in February. Waller was prevented from going immediately to its relief by a mutiny, and it was not the only one in the parliamentarian armies that winter. Even Cromwell's own regiment of horse, when ordered to Waller's support, refused to march without money, pistols and recruits, and Cromwell was hurriedly dispensed from attendance in Parliament so that he could restore discipline and join Waller in person. It was the old trouble: the Eastern Association, incensed at its army being kept so far from home, was stinting its pay and supplies. Parliament scored one major success in February when Colonel Mytton and the local Shropshire forces captured Shrewsbury, chief bastion of the upper Severn and for long a great royalist recruiting centre. But grave as this blow was, the royalists hoped to avenge it next month when Goring led a small but strong field army against Taunton. The little Puritan town was a running sore in the royalist west, and had already changed hands twice. Its Governor, Robert Blake, the hero of Lyme, had already stood a three months' siege in it last autumn, but this one was to be far more severe. Waller and Cromwell tried to come to its relief, but after a fortnight's skirmishing they were forced to retreat to the New Forest by the old troubles over pay and supplies.

But the royalists were having their own difficulties. Charles's losses in the north made him depend all the more on the south-western counties, but his hopes that the gentry would raise a new army for him were being wrecked by his own generals. Sir Richard Grenville was at loggerheads with Sir John Berke-ley, the Governor of Exeter, and both were objecting to taking orders from Goring, who was now bent on carving out an in-dependent command for himself in the west. Goring greatly offended Rupert by procuring a new commission whereby he was to receive orders only from the King's hand. At this time his bouts of drinking and debauchery were making him in-creasingly unreliable, and both his troops and Grenville's were committing such outrages upon the country that it could only long for deliverance from them. Something very significant occurred in March when Rupert went to the relief of Chester, which was then closely threatened by Brereton. Rupert drove the besiegers off to Middlewich, but then David Leslie appear-ed on the borders of Cheshire with 5000 Scots, sent by Leven to Brereton's relief. Brereton saw the chance of a major battle and tried to seize it. Within a day or two, however, Rupert was in rapid retreat; much as he disliked refusing a battle, a sudden rising in Herefordshire was threatening his whole rear. It had nothing to do with politics or religion. It was a spontaneous protest by simple countryfolk against all lawless armies that plundered and killed. These Clubmen, as they were called from their improvised weapons, cared far less what the armies fought for than for the hard-won produce of their fields and flocks and labour. Their leaders were mostly yeomen, with a few of the smaller gentry and even some clergymen. Some of them had firearms, and on 18 March 15,000 of them appeared before Hereford, fired on the defending troops and called on the citizens to let them into the town. Massey tried to enlist them for the Parliament, but they would have none of it. Rupert's cavalry dispersed them for the time being, but the Clubmen were to reappear in Dorset and other counties during the next few months. They were a portent that England would never be another Germany, to lie supine while marauding armies bled her white.

But penniless soldiers could not be stopped from helping themselves, and as the King's territory shrank he became less and less able to pay them. Discipline was slackening among the officers too; the royal forces were thick with colonels whose 'regiments' were no more than a troop or a company in strength, and who were left very much to their own devices to maintain them. Nor was Rupert's new command mending the quarrels among the commanders. His youth, his foreign birth,

Medal of the Earl of Manchester

his clashes of temperament with the courtiers at Oxford and their constant, subtle machinations against him all made his task harder; but so perhaps did the sardonic and pessimistic mood in which he entered the campaign of 1645. He saw knavery everywhere in the King's service, but he himself made enemies rather easily. Could more have been achieved by a general who was maturer, more suave and patient, better attuned to the vagaries of the Caroline gentry than this ardent, prickly young German prince? Possibly, but who else was there? In sheer drive and *élan* Rupert far outshone the rest;

no others had as much of the magic that puts an edge on soldiers' courage at the point of action. And no royalist general could end the evil of living at free quarter. Whoever commanded, unpaid armies would think less and less of saving their country, and more and more of simply living off it.

Charles I
From the painting by Sir Anthony van Dyck
The Royal Collection © 2000 HM Queen Elizabeth II

John Pym
Enlarged from the miniature by Samuel Cooper

Prince Rupert
From the portrait by Gerard Honthorst

Alexander Leslie
From a print of 1642

The Duke of Newcastle
From the portrait by Sir Anthony
van Dyck
From the Collection at Althorp

Sir Thomas Fairfax
Engraved, from the portrait by E. Bowers, for Joshua Sprigge's
'Anglia Rediviva', 1647

Oliver Cromwell
From the portrait by Robert Walker
National Portrait Gallery, London

The Earl of Manchester
Detail from the contemporary
portrait by Sir Peter Lely

Sir William Waller
Detail from the portrait
by Sir Peter Lely
Trustees of the Goodwood
Collection

Ralph Hopton
Detail of a contemporary
portrait
National Portrait
Gallery, London

Lord Goring (right), with the Earl of Newport
From a painting after Sir Anthony van Dyck
National Portrait Gallery, London

Musketeer

Infantry Officer

Pikeman

Drummer

Figurines from a staircase (c. 1638) of Cromwell House, Highgate

The Fairfax Jewel. Enamels (in a later setting), painted by P. Bordier, and presented by Parliament to General Fairfax on his victory at Naseby

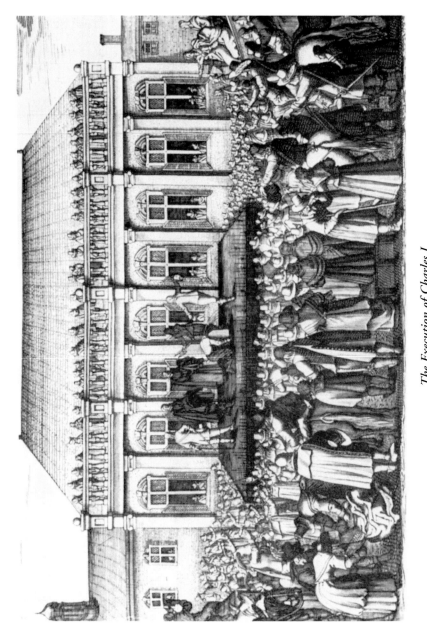

The Execution of Charles I

5

The New Model Army

IT WAS WELL for England that the means were found in 1645 for bringing the war to a decision, for the moral and material damage it was doing already threatened to leave deep scars. The damage was not to be reckoned only in terms of life, property and trade, or in crippling taxation and extortion, or in the break-up of families and communities. The war itself was getting harsher. Brutal and vindictive actions were commoner now, the slaughter in captured towns more indiscriminate, quarter less promptly granted. The courtesies at the highest level continued – as when Essex ordered the return of the Princes of Wales' captured falconer and hawk, or when the Newark garrison let Lady Fairfax and her retinue pass through on her way to join her husband, even though 'many muttered to let her good coach-horses pass' – but these were on the surface. In accordance with a barbarous parliamentary ordinance condemning to death any captured Irishman or English Catholics from Ireland, Mytton hanged thirteen of the prisoners he took at Shrewsbury, and Major-General Browne five officers who fell into his hands when Abingdon was attacked. Rupert retaliated against Mytton by hanging thirteen parliamentarian prisoners. When Essex protested, Rupert sent a long reply, drafted by Hyde, which expressed the fear 'that the English nation is in danger of destroying one another or (which is a kind of extirpation) of degenerating into such an animosity and cruelty, that all elements of charity, compassion and brotherly affection shall be extinguished'.

Parliament, in passing the New Model Ordinance, put it into Fairfax's hands to forge an instrument of total victory. But this was no bet on a certainty; indeed it seemed at the time a very bold step. It was taken in the teeth of such opposition that an early defeat or two could put the whole parliamentary cause at the peace party's mercy. During two or three months of transition, it meant leaving the military initiative to an enemy whose confidence had greatly recovered. And to build a new army out of such discouraging material as the old ones by this time offered was a task to challenge Fairfax and his officers to the utmost.

The strength of the New Model was fixed on paper at 22,000 men, but this modest target proved for many months beyond attainment. It was not hard to find its eleven cavalry regiments of 600 men each, or its single regiment of 1000 dragoons. Cromwell's horse of the Eastern Association, of whom Leslie had said at Marston Moor that 'Europe had no better soldiers', provided the nucleus, and Essex's and Waller's armies contributed in smaller proportions. The cavalry never lacked recruits; the trooper's pay of two shillings a day was three times that of the infantryman, and though it had to provide for his horse as well as himself, their joint needs were reckoned to be covered by about six shillings a week, so if pay were anything like regular he could live well. Many troopers brought their own horses to the service, and sometimes their simple armour – back, breast and headpiece or 'pot' – as well. The ranks of the cavalry were thus largely filled with men of some small substance, and most of them were both literate and highly aware of the issues of the war; whereas most foot-soldiers, when they subscribed petitions or attested evidence at courts-martial, could only make their mark.

The infantryman's eightpence a day was no more than the meanest labourer received, and it was subject to deductions for food, quarters and clothes. Low and irregular pay and hard conditions of service – bread or biscuit and cheese were the only rations normally issued in the field – largely explain why desertion was so rife and why impressment was needed to raise infantry recruits. So low had the foot sunk in the existing armies that 8460 fresh levies were needed to bring the New Model's infantry up to the target of 14,400. London and the county committees of the east and south-east were given quotas to raise, and few fulfilled them on time; even in June, a week before Naseby, those of the Eastern Association had furnished less than three-fifths of the men required of them. Even when raised it was a problem to prevent them from promptly deserting. The Kent contingent, for instance, mutinied so purposefully that a regular military operation was needed to bring it to heel. Nor were the old soldiers of the existing armies easy to embody. Those of Waller's who had not deserted were thoroughly mutinous, and the five regiments of Essex's scarcely less so until Skippon went down to Reading in person to promise them their arrears of pay.

It needed faith to believe that a few months would give this motley host the spirit of a proud and united army. The growing conviction that Parliament really cared for its needs, the leadership of officers who knew their jobs and cared deeply for their cause, above all the heady wine of victory – these would dry up the stream of deserters and breed a genuine pride of service. Later, when the tide of royalist defeats really set in, more and more of the captured royalist troops were to enlist under Fairfax, who declared in 1646 that they were the best common soldiers he had. Strong as the corporate spirit of the New Model was soon to become, it did not stem from the original convictions of the mass of its rank and file, most of whom were reluctant conscripts and not a few ex-royalists. Only the hard core of the cavalry, the men of the Eastern Association, were devoted from trooper to general to an ideology – and not to any single creed or sect, but to a belief in the common purpose of all God's saints and a conviction that they were fighting the Lord's battles. This leaven would work in time through the army as a whole, to mould its revolutionary dynamism and inspire its unique sense of mission. But though eleven of its twenty-four original regimental commanders were drawn from the Eastern Association, all this lay in the future. Fairfax and his officers had plenty to do in March and April to form an army at all out of the raw material which was coming slowly under their hands. Old units had to be reorganized and taught to accept new leadership; new ones had to be armed, equipped and trained in a matter of weeks. To their arms, equipment and training we shall now briefly turn.

The infantry regiments of the New Model, twelve in all, had each a strength of 1200 men, organized in ten companies. For the first time an English army wore something like uniform throughout. All the infantry wore the red coats that had become prevalent in the Eastern Association, each regiment being distinguished by the colour of its facings. They marched in shoes, not boots, with knee-length stockings pulled up over the legs of their breeches. The musket and the pike were their weapons, in the proportion of two to one in every company. The pikemen considered themselves a cut above the musketeers, not so much by reason of the universal military tendency to associate social prestige with obsolescent weapons as because they were usually the tallest and strongest men in their companies. They had to be. Earlier they had worn a corselet and the ridged iron helmet called a combe-cap, but this armour was falling out of use because a pike sixteen feet long with a heavy iron head, together with a sword and the rest of their kit and rations, was about as much as they could carry. The pike's main role was to repel cavalry charges, against which musketeers, as yet without bayonets, were almost defenceless. But when two infantry forces met in head-on clash, the pikemen, their weapons levelled against their opponents, sustained the first shock; they fought it out 'at push of pike'. Before that there was usually a brief halt at short range for the musketeers to deliver a volley or two, but when it came to hand-to-hand fighting the musketeers generally relied more on clubbing with their musket-butts than on the cheap, untrustworthy swords which were issued to common soldiers.

The matchlock musket with which they were armed was a crude and cumbersome weapon. It necessitated carrying a length of match (cord boiled in vinegar) which had to be kept lighted whenever there was any prospect of action or surprise, which in rain was very difficult. Its wide-bored barrel, three to four feet long, made it very heavy, and a long rest with a crook at one end and a spike at the other was only just going out of use. To fire it, first a charge of powder – the soldier usually carried a dozen ready prepared on a bandolier over his shoulder – had to be rammed down the muzzle, and then the heavy lead ball (which was apt to roll out again if aimed low). Next, when a short length of lighted match had been fixed in the cock, a pinch of fine powder was placed as a primer in the pan, into which the cock snapped down when the trigger was pulled. Wind made priming hazardous, and there was always a danger when firing in close ranks that a spark from another musket might explode the primer prematurely, or even the charges in the soldier's bandolier. Musketeers usually fought six ranks deep, and practised an elaborate drill whereby the front rank, after firing, was successively replaced by the others, with pieces primed and ready, so that each could reload before its turn came again. But the New Model also mastered the newer Swedish practice whereby three ranks could fire a 'salvee' simultaneously, the first kneeling, the second stooping, the rear standing. The musket could kill at 400 yards or more, but for any real accuracy fire was usually withheld until the enemy was within 100 or 150 yards. The far more efficient flintlock mechanism, which needed no match, was familiar in pistols and sporting guns, but was still too scarce and dear for infantry muskets. Flintlocks however were issued to two special foot companies, in tawny coats, which were used to guard the artillery and ammunition.

The famous New Model cavalry wore, beneath their 'back and breast' armour, buff coats of thick leather which could cost up to £10 – at least as much as the average trooper's mount. Their iron headpieces were highly functional and curiously menacing. They were uniformly armed with a straight sword and a pair of pistols, and though technically classed as harquebusiers it was by now only officers who carried the shorter, lighter flintlock gun called a harquebus or carbine. Neither cuirassiers, the heavy cavalry in full armour of which Haselrig's regiment of 'lobsters' had provided a quaint example in the earlier Civil War campaigns, nor lancers, who scarcely survived in the west except in the forces of Spain and Scotland, had any place in Fairfax's army.

Cavalry tactics were in transition when the Civil War began. Best known then was the Dutch drill, which relied on fire-power rather than shock and cold steel. Dutch cavalry attacked by trotting forward at least five ranks deep, halting close to the enemy, discharging its pistols rank by rank (each riding round to the rear after it had fired), and then generally withdrawing. This was how Essex's cavalry had fought in some earlier actions of the war. But Gustavus Adolphus had ranged his horse in only three ranks, and taught it to charge swiftly and charge home, reserving its fire until right in the enemy's midst. Rupert had followed these Swedish tactics of charging home sword in hand from Edgehill onwards, and so devastatingly successful were they that his opponents, Cromwell among the first, soon copied them. By the time the New Model was formed they had completely supplanted the Dutch practice. Rupert's cavalry and Cromwell's did not differ essentially in arms, armour, mounts, or even tactics, though Sir Charles Firth was probably right in his impression that Rupert generally charged at a greater pace than Cromwell, who was content with 'a pretty round trot', and relied less on sheer momentum than on hacking and shooting it out with sword and pistol. Cromwell could certainly control and order his men after action was joined in a manner Rupert seldom achieved.

It so happens that artillery played little part in our three battles. But there were others in which it was more important, and the army's fifty or so field guns accounted for a considerable proportion of the horses – more than a thousand – which were needed to draw its train and baggage. They ranged from the demi-culverin, with a ball of nine to twelve pounds, down through the saker to the little three-pounder drake. They were usually charged (highly dangerously) straight from the powder-barrel with an iron ladle, and few could fire more than fifteen shots an hour. Beyond about three hundred paces most were grossly inaccurate, and sieges apart they were only really effective against massed formations at point-blank range.

Apart from a few gunners, the New Model had practically none of the specialist personnel which makes up so large a part of modern armies – no corps of sappers or engineers, for instance, but only a single company of pioneers who were mere unskilled labourers. Medical services, like the whole commissariat, were rudimentary. Apart from three or four general medical officers attached to headquarters, there were only the regimental surgeons, paid about the same as ensigns and seldom known to the Royal College of Physicians, each aided by two surgeon's mates. The spiritual health of this army, soon to be famous (or notorious) for praying and preaching, was still more sketchily provided for, with very few regimental chaplains and most of the work done by half-a-dozen ministers attached to headquarters. Most of these were of the ultra-Puritan persuasion known as Antinomian, and they were extraordinarily zealous. Naturally they made a special point of preaching on the eve of battle. The Eastern Association cavalry had long been used to hearing officers, and troopers too, preach and expound the Scriptures, but the rest of the army did not at once take to such practices. When Colonel Pickering, a former Eastern Association officer, attempted to preach a sermon to his newly-formed regiment of foot it promptly mutinied. Parliament then immediately passed an ordinance forbidding any but ordained ministers to preach. But though it was sent to Fairfax with instructions to see it strictly enforced it was widely disregarded, and in the last year's fighting many a church pulpit was taken over by officers or soldiers.

It was a commonplace of royalist and even Presbyterian propaganda that the officers of the New Model, like all fanatics and sectaries, were men of low birth. As Denzil Holles put it (and he should have known better), 'most of the colonels are tradesmen, brewers, tailors, goldsmiths, shoemakers and the like'. But Fairfax's officers were very far from being all sectaries, and of the thirty-seven original colonels and general officers only seven were not gentlemen by birth, and nine came of noble families. If there were fewer gentlemen than in the King's armies, it was partly because the New Model imposed a more rational proportion between officers and other ranks. Though some junior officers were humbly born, many were drawn from the lesser gentry; large-scale promotion from the ranks still lay in the future. And in case it does still need to be said, the popular idea of parliamentarian officers sharply distinguished from royalists by their cropped heads and black Puritan garb is a myth. Almost every portrait we have of them shows them wearing their hair long, and Fairfax at Marston Moor was by no means alone in discovering how easily a parliamentarian could be mistaken for a royalist, or vice versa.

Though the New Model was to make 1645 the year of decision, nothing seemed less likely during the first spring months of campaigning. The strategy of both sides was so fumbling and changeable that the campaigns of the two previous years are lucid and logical by comparison. We must simplify a complicated story as best we can to explain how a decisive battle came to be fought at all.

The key to the situation at first lay in Goring's threat to Taunton and Brereton's to Chester, for Brereton soon resumed his siege with stronger forces. Chester was vital to the King's schemes for bringing over an Irish army, and in mid-April Rupert and Maurice set out in strength from Evesham on a second attempt to relieve it. Charles prepared to join them with the artillery train and the rest of the royal army from Oxford. When Cromwell returned from the west with his cavalry brigade, to lay down his commission and hand over his troops to Fairfax, he was promptly sent off with them again to threaten Oxford and keep the King's forces occupied. This he did by ten days' hard hitting at Oxford's outlying defences to the north and west, and by driving off all he could of the draught horses which Charles would need for moving his guns – and Charles needed 400. The King had to change his plans. Instead of marching to join Rupert he had to summon the Prince to join him, bringing the horses he needed. More than that, he recalled Goring and all his cavalry to Oxford.

As Goring rode eastward to the King's rescue, the New Model set off westward on its first march, which was to relieve Taunton. The gallant little Puritan town deserved well, of

course, and was still besieged by Goring's infantry and Grenville's local forces. But it was foolish to commit the Parliament's one field army so far from the King's main forces, and
so long before it was really ready. Fairfax had only 11,000 men
as yet; much of his infantry was very raw and his best cavalry
was absent under Cromwell. Then when a week's hard marching had carried them westward of Blandford they were all
recalled, except for six regiments under Colonel Welden which
were to go on and succour Taunton as best they could. Parliament had decided on 5 May that the concentration of the
King's, the Princes' and Goring's forces about Oxford was
altogether too threatening. So it was, but by the time Fairfax
got back to Newbury his troops were in worse shape than when
they set out. They had marched a whole fortnight through an
early heatwave with only one day's rest, they were temporarily
exhausted and their shoes were worn out.

It was the sort of price that had to be paid for subjecting
the army to remote control from Westminster. When its orders
had often to be debated by both Houses before being sent off
by the Committee of Both Kingdoms, when intelligence came
in and instructions went out only as fast as a man could ride
a horse, Fairfax too often received instructions which seemed
only relevant to the enemy's last move but one. Control by
committee also tended towards a defensive rather than an
offensive mentality, especially now that Essex and Manchester
were back at Westminster. And military strategy was apt to
become just one of the pieces in the political chess-game between Independents and Presbyterians or English and Scots.
One somehow doubts whether Fairfax's task became any easier
when Parliament sent four of its members to join him in the
field and participate in all his councils of war.

On 8 May, the day Fairfax began his return march, Charles
and Rupert led their forces to Stow-on-the-Wold for a general
rendezvous. There Sir Marmaduke Langdale brought in the
northern cavalry, and Lord Astley the large part of the royal
infantry that had been wintering in Gloucestershire. In all,
Charles mustered at least 5000 foot and 6000 horse – as many

as Fairfax and far stronger in cavalry. But where were they to march? Dissension among their commanders broke out in a council of war, held in that same little hill-top town where Essex a year ago had taken his disastrous decision to part from Waller and march into the west. Stow-on-the-Wold now became the scene of an almost equally unhappy choice.

This choice was broadly between the north and the west – between relieving Chester without delay and then tackling the Scots, or reducing Taunton and crushing the New Noddle, as the royalists contemptuously called it, as thoroughly as Essex had been crushed last summer. Charles favoured the north because ever since last September Montrose and his little Highland bands had been winning a series of victories which seemed to promise a great royalist resurgence in Scotland. The rout of the Covenanters at Tippermuir and Aberdeen had been followed by the slaughter of the Campbells at Inverlochy, under Argyle's own impotent gaze. Leven's army in England had already been bled of some of its best regiments to save their homelands from the clansmen's fearful rapine, and now the Scottish Estates were calling home more. After Inverlochy Montrose believed he had Scotland at his feet, and he had invited his King to come north and place himself at the head of the loyal subjects whom he now expected to flock to the royal banner. Charles was enchanted. As for Rupert, he would know better than to commit the King's main forces to Scotland while the New Model remained undefeated behind him, but the weakening of Leven opened a bright hope of avenging Marston Moor, saving Carlisle and recovering the north. Langdale's horse had relieved Pontefract two months ago, inflicting a severe defeat on the elder Fairfax, and since then his officers had petitioned forcefully to be sent back to Yorkshire. It might indeed be ripe for the winning. As for Fairfax's threat to the west, a swift strike northward in full strength would soon draw it off.

But Langdale was Rupert's only supporter in pressing for the north. Goring was too intent on an independent command in the west to have anything to do with it, and the majority in the council of war were for the west too. Certainly, if the King's united forces had continued westward, cut off Fairfax's retreat from Blandford and brought him to battle as he was, they might have struck a blow from which the war party at Westminster might never have recovered. Either the northern or the western design could have been formidable; the essential was to pursue one or the other with all the force and vigour that could be summoned. Instead, Charles acquiesced in a wretched compromise. He and Rupert were to march north with the main army, while Goring returned to Taunton with his 3000 horse and a new commission, large enough in itself and soon extended to the chief command of all the western forces. Rupert let him go the more easily because he feared that if he had to bear the company of both Goring and Digby, who were now as thick as thieves, he would find his own author-ity undermined at every turn. But this parting was the begin-ning of the King's defeat.

However, for the moment its consequences were mitigated by equal blundering on the other side. As Charles and Rupert advanced towards Droitwich their threat to the north became clear, and the obvious counter to it would have been to send Fairfax after them. Instead the Committee of Both Kingdoms appealed to Leven, not for the first time, to march south with all speed, and ordered all the local forces it could call upon – 1500 of Brereton's from Cheshire, 2000 of the elder Fairfax's from Yorkshire, and more from Lancashire, Derbyshire, Not-tinghamshire and Staffordshire – to join the Scots at whatever rendezvous Leven and Fairfax should agree upon. Cromwell's cavalry brigade and Major-General Browne's motley force from Abingdon were to advance northward together through Warwickshire, watching the King's right flank. But the New Model was not to be involved.

It was a crazy plan, and it never had a chance of saving the siege of Chester, which Brereton was forced to abandon on 17 May. Leven, who had only recently left Newcastle and was marching by very easy stages towards Ripon, was disgruntled with his English allies and reluctant to leave Scotland far behind him while Montrose's Highlanders ravaged unchecked. Under pressure, he appointed a rendezvous with the various English forces for 22 May at Barlow Moor, just south of Manchester, but it remained to be seen whether the northern and midland counties would be prepared to denude themselves of the troops which defended them. Though Brereton sent confident intelligence – unfounded, as it proved – that the King meant to send a 'flying army' to join Montrose, no one knew for certain where Charles and Rupert would strike next. In fact, the patchwork northern army planned on paper at Westminster never looked like coming into existence.

Behind these feeble plans lay a sharp rift between the English and Scots in the Committee of Both Kingdoms. The Scottish commissioners naturally resented that their own army should be expected to bear the brunt of the King's main offensive, and pressed hard that the New Model should go to Leven's support so that they might engage the enemy together with the same superiority that had won Marston Moor. After six days' wrangling this was put to a special committee of the two Houses and defeated by a single vote. As a compromise, a mere brigade of 2500 horse and dragoons from the New Model was sent to join the Scots under Colonel Vermuyden.

It was the Independents who were so opposed to sending the New Model north, for they had in mind another task for it which they hoped would win the war without giving the Scots a share in the decisive victory. The stroke they planned was no less than the capture of Oxford, the King's headquarters and the seat of his government. This juicy carrot was dangled before their noses by Viscount Savile, a privy councillor of the King who had been arrested at Oxford for treason in January, and released only on pledging himself to depart at once for France. Instead he had crawled back to Westminster, to entertain his more gullible fellow-peers with assurances that if all the monarchy itself could be guaranteed, Goring would bring over all his cavalry to force Charles to a negotiated peace, while William Legge, the Governor of Oxford, would open the gates to a besieging army. Lord Saye and Sele swallowed these unlikely stories and carried the Committee of Both Kingdoms with him. On 17 May the two Houses endorsed its plans. The reducing of Oxford was to be the 'main action' of the campaign, and not only the New Model but all the available local forces in the south were to be concentrated upon it. It was a classic instance of how politics could bedevil strategy; only civilian minds could have been blind to the folly of putting so much into a long and elaborate siege while the enemy had two armies, the King's and Goring's, unbeaten in the field.

Let us see how both sides' armies stood on 22 May, the day that Fairfax, Cromwell and Browne obediently joined forces before Oxford. It was also the day on which the northern and midland contingents should have come in to Leven on Barlow Moor. The rendezvous was a fiasco; Brereton found only 1300 English troops there instead of the 7000 summoned, and no Scots at all. Leven, in fact, was marching farther away every day. At Ripon, the day before, he had announced that he would march for Lancashire, not by the direct route through Skipton which Rupert had taken last summer, but by an immense detour to the north through Bowes and Brough and into Westmorland. His real reason lay in a fresh victory by Montrose at Auldearn, capped by Brereton's intelligence that Charles meant to send his champion strong reinforcements from England. Leven would not leave Scotland 'naked', he said, and he felt little compunction now on account of his English allies. He complained with some reason that his army was starved of money and supplies, while the New Model, which he detested on political and religious grounds, was getting all that Parliament could bestow. He was stung when his critics pointed out that he had done nothing since Marston Moor but capture Newcastle, and that that was seven months ago. After all, he had had to send nine regiments back to Scotland, five were tied down before Carlisle and as many more garrisoning Newcastle, and his casualties had not been replaced by fresh recruits. But Leven's virtual retreat meant that there was nothing in all Lancashire that could stem the royalists' advance.

Charles and Rupert had now reached Market Drayton, and there Lord Byron joined them. Byron urged them to seize their chance and push on northward while the way lay wide open, but the decision went against him. Rupert did not of course know yet of the threat to Oxford, but he did know that the New Model had returned to Newbury, and he took this to presage a challenge somewhere in the Midlands. It was a challenge he meant to accept. Already, three days ago, he had sent urgent orders to Goring at Taunton to march with all his horse and foot and rejoin the King and himself at Market Harborough. He hoped to pick up Charles Gerrard with about 3000 Welsh levies in the same area, and had ordered the Newark garrison to have a considerable cavalry force ready to join him. It must have been hard to resist the chance to raise the King's banner again in the north-west and drive the Scots out of England, but it would have been a gamble to leave the New Model unchecked in his rear, and if all went well in the midlands the Vale of York would still afford a better route north than the evil roads of Lancashire.

So Charles marched eastward with his army through Stone and Tutbury to Burton-on-Trent, encouraging his soldiers by sharing some of their hardships and refusing to take his coach when the weather turned foul. On 25 May Digby wrote to Oxford in high confidence, counting on Goring, Gerrard and the Newark horse joining them within a few days and looking forward to 'a battle of all for all' inside a month, probably somewhere near Leicester. Next day came the first news that Oxford was besieged. There was alarm in the town that its provisions would not hold out; worse, there was no sign yet of Goring, whom Rupert expected to have reached the Oxford area by now. Goring in fact was at Bath. He had replied to Rupert's pressing orders by promising to march as soon as he had taken Taunton, which he undertook to reduce in a matter of days. But his debauches were now occupying him for three or four days at a time, while his men deserted and Taunton's defenders brought in provisions through his lines with impunity. Fresh orders were now sent to him to march with all strength and speed, to relieve the pressure on Oxford. If it could be defended for even six weeks, Digby wrote to him, the King had every hope of relieving Pontefract, recovering Yorkshire and returning with 'a gallant army indeed' to deal with Oxford's besiegers. But all depended on Goring playing his part; the King and Rupert would expect his reply at Leicester, where they hoped to meet Gerrard and his Welshmen in three days' time.

Against Leicester they now marched. It was the centre of quite a group of parliamentary garrisons, and an attack there might draw off Fairfax. It was a rich town too, whose plunder would be a spur to the King's ill-paid soldiers. The Committee of Both Kingdoms was already worried by the royal army's wheel to the east; it sent Cromwell to the Isle of Ely to raise the trained bands of the Eastern Association, and ordered Vermuyden's brigade and the Yorkshire and north midlands local forces to gather with all speed at Nottingham. But nothing would make it call off the siege of Oxford, even when Leicester was directly threatened. Not that Oxford showed any signs of yielding; indeed the investing forces had received some sharp checks, and their siege artillery had not even arrived yet from Windsor. It needed Leicester's agony to jerk the men at Westminster to their senses, and to bring on that decisive battle in which they seemed to have so little faith.

6

Naseby

THERE WAS no operation in which Rupert so grimly ex-
celled as the sudden assault of a fortified town. On 28 May
he was joined by Sir Richard Willys, the Governor of Newark,
with 1200 horse, and next day he had Leicester invested. At
one o'clock on the 30th, as soon as his first siege guns were in
position, he summoned the town to surrender. It was in poor
shape to resist. Its Governor, Lord Grey of Groby, was away,
and its garrison and fortifications had been neglected. The
walls were made vulnerable by suburban buildings which no
one had liked to pull down, and the outer defences were drawn
far too wide. For Leicester had only 1500 defenders, and little
more than a third of them were regulars. Indeed, had not
two officers of the New Model, Colonel Sir Robert Pye and
Major Innes, just arrived almost by chance with 200 dragoons,
there might have been little or no resistance. As it was the
frightened county committee and town corporation sent out a
trumpeter to ask for a night's grace to consider their reply, and
to protest at Rupert's continuing to raise his batteries while the
parley was in progress. This tried the Prince's temper, for he
had not come to waste time on the formalities of a siege. He
told their man he would lay him by the heels if he came with
another such message, and gave them just a quarter of an hour
to make up their minds.

At three o'clock six great guns opened up against the quarter
called the Newark, where a sort of citadel had been improvised.
Three hours' bombardment opened a wide breach in it, and
though men and women toiled under fire through the evening
to raise new works within the old, Rupert ordered a general
assault that same night. It was launched about midnight from
several points at once, but chiefly against the exposed Newark.
For over two hours soldiers, citizens and even their women-

folk shared a desperate resistance. Within the breach Pye and
Innes and their men repulsed attack after attack, but as
Rupert's infantry fell back his cavalry behind drove them on
again. The breach was only yielded when the walls were scaled
in other quarters, but even then, when the royalist cavalry poured into the town, the defenders contested its advance street by
street and made a final fierce stand in the market place before
throwing down their arms. Not all received quarter, for the
royalists had lost about thirty officers, and this resistance after
the town had been entered exasperated them. The sack which
ensued was terrible; it did not spare the humblest cottage or
distinguish between friend and foe. When the Mayor came to
attend the King to church next day he found that even his mace
was gone, and it was said that no royalist soldier captured between Leicester and Naseby had less than forty shillings about
him.

The shock of Leicester hit London very hard. A loud outcry went up against the Scots, and less fairly against the New
Model and those who had brought it into being. But the lesson
was taken to heart. Sunday though it was, the Committee of
Both Kingdoms met on 1 June and at once recommended to
Parliament that the New Model should take the field. Next day
Fairfax had his marching orders for Buckingham. Soon after
he was at last freed from the Committee's leading-strings and
told simply to follow the King's movements as he judged best
on the spot. 'All these things', commented a newspaper when
the New Model set forth after the enemy at last, 'will seem
like dreams to many men; but they must understand we will be
no more a-dreaming; the business of Leicester hath awakened
us'. But this confidence was not very widely shared; the month
of June opened in London to a mood of pessimism and recrimination. 'Never hardly did any army go forth to war', wrote
a parliamentary chronicler, 'who had less of the confidence of
their own friends, or were more the objects of the contempt of
their enemies.'

After a few days' rest at Leicester the King's council of war,
not knowing that Oxford was already free from danger, decided

that the first task must be to relieve it. Rupert was disgusted with the decision – a plot, he called it – but he was overborne by the courtiers, led by Digby and Jack Ashburnham and backed by the frightened pleas of their friends (not least the ladies) in Oxford. Not that it was intended to engage the New Model precipitately, for the King's army was depleted now by the garrison it had had to find for Leicester, besides its casualties in the assault and the large numbers of soldiers who had simply made off to dispose of their booty. Willys took 400 of his cavalry back to Newark, too, leaving the rest to join the northern horse under Langdale. Charles himself reckoned, perhaps pessimistically, that out of about 11,000 men he had led against Leicester, he could now call on scarcely 4000 foot and 3500 horse. The plan was to make for Market Harborough, there to gather in stragglers and await intelligence both of Oxford's predicament and the expected reinforcements which Goring and Gerrard were supposed to be bringing. But when Langdale's horse heard that they were not to march north they broke into open mutiny. Despite Langdale's own pleas for obedience and Charles's promise as a King that he would march for Yorkshire as soon as Oxford was safe, they rode off towards Newark, and were only with difficulty brought back to the army before it marched into Market Harborough on 5 June.

That same day, Fairfax set off from before Oxford. He started badly, with an attack on Boarstall House which was repelled with some loss. But three long days' marches took him just north of Newport Pagnell, where Vermuyden's brigade came in to him and brought his strength up to about 13,000, including 5500 horse and dragoons. Apart from shifting his quarters a few miles west to Stony Stratford, Fairfax made no further move before the 11th.

The royalists too were temporarily immobile, less than twenty-five miles away. They had advanced another dozen miles to Daventry on the 7th, but there they stuck for six full days. To save Oxford from being starved into surrender, they had been scouring a great tract of countryside for sheep and cattle, and the vast flocks and herds they collected were driven off southward on the 8th with a convoy of 1200 horse – about a third of all Rupert's cavalry. He had to wait at Daventry till the convoy returned, which it did not do until the night of 11/12 June. This is one of the mysteries of the campaign, for Rupert certainly knew no later than the 7th that the siege of Oxford had been raised and that Fairfax was on the march. Why then did he cripple himself to provide a garrison which could now quite well forage for itself? Whatever the reason, he sacrificed the initiative he had so far held, and also the chance of getting out of Fairfax's reach until Gerrard's Welshmen and further reinforcements from Newark could be called in. The two opposed armies were not ignorant of each other's whereabouts, as Clarendon thought. Fairfax had excellent intelligence of the royalists' movements from Sir Samuel Luke, the Governor of Newport Pagnell, which he was able to confirm on the 8th when a cavalry patrol brought in some of Langdale's troopers as prisoners. And Rupert must have realized the New Model's proximity not later than the 10th, when Fairfax sent a trumpeter to the King's headquarters to negotiate the exchange of some of the Leicester prisoners.

There was better reason for Fairfax's shorter pause about Stony Stratford, for much needed to be done before his army was ready to fight. About its will to fight there was no doubt; the question he put to his council of war on the 8th was simply how best to engage the enemy. Not the only question, however, for the post of Lieutenant-General, carrying the command of the horse, was still unfilled. Since the backbone of his cavalry was formed from the veteran regiments of the Eastern Association, there was a warm and unanimous response when Fairfax himself proposed Cromwell. Colonel Hammond posted to Westminster to ask Parliament to appoint him; the Commons agreed at once, but the Lords could not be brought to concur. They had not forgiven Cromwell for his attack on Manchester, and they cannot have relished the busy propaganda which the Independent-inspired London news-sheets were making for him. But for Fairfax, for Cromwell and for the scores of officers who longed to welcome back an old comrade and a great soldier, the Commons' authority was enough.

Meanwhile there was urgent work to do. It fell to Skippon, as Major-General, to organize the regiments into brigades of horse and foot so that each commander should know his station when the army formed up on the field. This was quite normally a last-minute, *ad hoc* arrangement in the armies of the Civil War, which knew no permanent units larger than the regiment. But training of a more elementary kind was also needed, for many of Fairfax's recruits were not even armed until a large consignment of muskets and pistols overtook him on the march from Oxford. They were not taking kindly to discipline, especially now they found themselves on short rations. The fact was that the countryfolk had grown so 'malignant', what with the fall in the Parliament's stock after Leicester and the proximity of the King's forces, that the county committee had the utmost difficulty in bringing in provisions. But if bread was short there was always beer. 'I think these New Modellers knead all their dough with ale,' wrote Sir Samuel Luke to his father, 'for I never see so many drunk in my life in so short a time.' 'An ungodly crew', he pronounced them, 'grown so wild since they came near the enemy that devout Christians cannot abide them.' He granted that the men were 'extraordinary personable, well dressed and well paid, but the officers you will hardly distinguish from common soldiers'.[1] But then Luke was a strong Presbyterian, and looked upon this allegedly Independent host with jaundiced eyes.

Back in London, tension was building up at the prospect of a crucial trial of strength. The Commons met at eight instead of nine on the morning of 11 June, to devote an hour to intercessions for the army. As a minister from the Assembly of Divines led them in prayer, the army itself was just gathering for the final advance that would commit it irrevocably to battle. It was a day of foul weather, and the downpour was at its height when the troops, having left their scattered quarters very early, formed up at Hanslope. Thence they toiled along

1. *British Museum, Egerton MSS. 786, fols.* 30, 33, 70. Luke was the original of Samuel Butler's Sir Hudibras.

little-frequented country lanes to Wootton, just short of Northampton, but the way was cheered for them by news that Cromwell, after mustering several thousand of the Eastern Association's trained bands, was within a day's march and only waiting for some men from Essex before catching them up. Fairfax
sent him orders to join the army with all speed, whether or not
he could bring his East Anglians with him. Charles and Rupert
had no idea that evening that the New Model was within a
dozen miles of them, even though a royalist party, hiding in
Whittlewood Forest near Stony Stratford, had captured some
of its stragglers. Perhaps the rain made their cavalry slack in
patrolling. It was not until late in the following afternoon that
they realized their danger, when Fairfax's forward cavalry
clashed with their outposts only two miles from Daventry. The
King was hunting in Fawsley Park when the news was brought
to him. Fairfax had been probing westward cautiously from
about Northampton, knowing that the royalists had been preparing a strong position on Borough Hill, an eminence crowned
with ancient earthworks just east of Daventry. The surprise
he achieved, with his opponents relaxed and dispersed and
their horses at grass, was more than he could have dared hope
for, but the day was too far spent and his infantry too far behind for any general attack that evening.

As quickly as they could be roused, the King's forces assembled on Borough Hill, and there they stood to their arms till
daybreak. The New Model quartered about Kislingbury, but
for Fairfax there was no sleep that night. He was in the saddle
from midnight till four in the morning, anxious to check his
security against a possible night attack on his quarters. But
when the first sentry stopped him he found himself without
the password. The man was not to be talked into divulging it,
and kept his commander-in-chief standing in the rain until he
got his captain's permission to let him pass. He did not go un-
rewarded. Fairfax however was not losing a night's rest merely
to keep his troops on their toes; he wanted to see what he could
of the ground and the enemy for himself. He rode forward
until at about three o'clock, from near Flore, he could descry

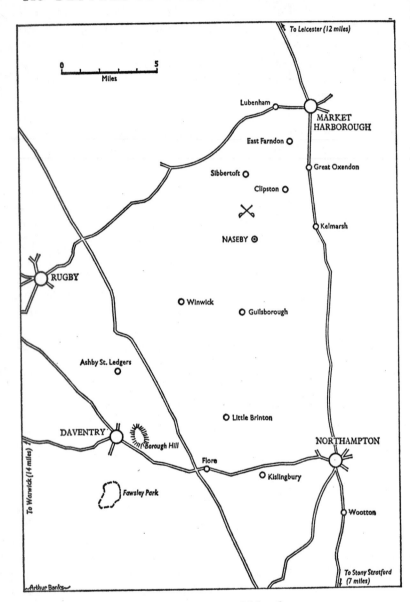

The Environs of Naseby

the dim outlines of Borough Hill three or four miles away. There he could see many fires twinkling, so many that he thought the soldiers must be burning their huts prior to moving off. Two hours later Scoutmaster-General Watson confirmed that they were indeed in retreat. He also brought in a still more interesting piece of news in the shape of an intercepted letter from Goring to Rupert, begging him not to fight a battle till he could join him, but declaring he could not possibly leave the west just yet. So that was one army Fairfax need not fear. At six he held a council of war, and needless to say its decision was to pursue the enemy and bring him to battle. Even as it sat, a mighty shout of joy from the cavalry quarters announced the arrival of Cromwell, who rode in with about 700 horse.

Rather than fight at once against heavy odds, Charles and Rupert had decided to retreat through Market Harborough and Melton Mowbray to Belvoir Castle, where they could draw in reinforcements from Newark and other midland garrisons. As a feint, they first marched westwards for some miles along the Warwick road, leaving a heavy screen of cavalry to check any pursuit, before they wheeled north-east towards Harborough. But strong detachments of Fairfax's – now Cromwell's – horse under Colonel Ireton and Major Harrison kept touch with their movements, and the body of the New Model followed much closer than they imagined upon their right flank. There was irony in the choice of Ireton and Harrison to harry the King's retreat, for little more than three years later these very two officers were to play the major part in bringing the army to the pitch of putting him on trial for his life, and both were to sign his death warrant. In a wide arc the army marched that day, through Little Brinton, Ashby St Ledgers and Winwick, before it quartered for the night at Guilsborough. Neither Rupert at his headquarters in Harborough, nor Charles as he retired to rest at Lubenham, evidently knew how close their pursuers were; anyhow they had left some troops at Naseby to cover their rear. But Ireton fell on these troops as they took their ease at supper or quoits, and he captured many prisoners. The rest carried the alarm swiftly back. The King, called from his bed at eleven at night, hastened into Harborough, roused Rupert in his turn and held a midnight council of war.

The only question was whether to turn and fight, or pull out hastily and make for the shelter of Leicester. Either course was hazardous; Fairfax and Cromwell would be so close on their tails that the royal forces would be lucky to get away without a mauling, and the retreat might turn into ignominious flight. Besides, if they put off fighting too long they might yet be caught between Fairfax and the Scots. But Rupert was against giving battle, and when Rupert could bring himself to decline a challenge from an enemy almost within cannon-shot, amateur tacticians should have known to give way. But it was Digby and Ashburnham whose voices once more swayed the council of war, and made a futile point of honour of scorning to retreat. They had swallowed all the fatuous royalist gossip about the New Model's morale. Their own troops were still elated with the victory at Leicester, they argued; Fairfax's had nothing behind them but the fiasco of Oxford and a bloody check at Boarstall House. Better to strike now, before the moral advantage (a very dubious one in view of the temper of Langdale's horse) was reversed. And when Charles himself could retail absurd stores of murderous affrays between Fairfax's men and Cromwell's, and of Fairfax and Browne falling on each other with cudgels, who was he to uphold his commander-in-chief against his silly, sanguine courtiers?

His troops were roused at two in the morning, but since many had to be brought in from surrounding villages it was some hours before they were all mustered in Harborough. Fairfax's men were astir equally early. Unlike their opponents, however, they had quartered for the night knowing they must march out to battle in the morning, and had remained sufficiently concentrated to be on the move when the sun rose at a quarter to four. Little more than an hour later they made their rendezvous at Naseby. The village lies high, just backward of the brow of a broad hill which commands wide views of the rolling country to the north, where the enemy might at any moment appear. But would he? Fairfax knew from his scouts

that the royalists were in Harborough, but what he could not
know yet was whether they would come out and fight or go
on retreating. Soon, however, the question was answered by the
appearance of large numbers of their cavalry on a ridge four
miles away. So the King would give battle; the next task was
to find the best ground on which to meet him.

Rupert, guessing that his enemy might have the start on him
and not knowing how soon he might have to face an attack,
wisely drew up his forces on the first piece of ground south
of Harborough to afford a sound defensive position. His choice
was the obvious one: the straight ridge, just over a mile long
and 500 feet high, which runs between East Farndon and Great
Oxendon. The Naseby ridge, being rather higher, formed the
skyline to the south; his cavalry vanguard plainly saw the New
Model horse on it, and was seen by them. But by about 8
o'clock, when he had his army ranged along the ridge in
'battalia', Rupert could see his opponents no more. To visualize
the ground as he saw it, we have to erase in our minds the typically English checkerboard of small fields, thick hedges, frequent trees and scattered woods and spinneys which covers it
today. Its general picture was rather of ill-drained, furze-
dotted heath, varied here and there by the great open fields
within which the midland villagers ploughed their narrow
strip-holdings before the days of large-scale enclosure. But
open as the view was, between Rupert's ridge and the Naseby
one there rolled a series of lesser undulations which were quite
sufficient to conceal an army as soon as it moved down off the
heights. So, while prayers were said at the head of his troops,
Rupert sent his scoutmaster, Ruce, to find out what was happening ahead. If Ruce always scamped his job as he did that
morning, we know why royalist intelligence was so feeble
during this campaign. He came back to report that he had been
forward two or three miles but had neither seen nor heard of
the rebels. Rupert did not believe him; impatiently he rode
off with his life guard to make his own reconnaissance. But
though he soon sighted the enemy van, its behaviour puzzled
him, for Cromwell's cavalry was moving not forward but back.

Fairfax had evidently decided that he could not be sure of Rupert's engaging him if he stood on the Naseby ridge, and had advanced to a position forward of the one he finally adopted, and somewhat lower. His army actually began to deploy over it. Its front was covered by ground which, perhaps through being waterlogged, would prove a severe obstacle to attacking cavalry – so severe that Cromwell, when he saw it, thought that it might defeat their whole object of bringing on a battle. 'Let us, I beseech you,' he said, 'draw back to yonder hill, which will encourage the enemy to charge us, which they cannot do in that place without absolute ruin.' His advice was followed. Just where this incident took place, the vague and even conflicting evidence we have makes it impossible to establish. Historians have discussed the point elaborately, but always on the supposition that the New Model had been advancing along the road from Naseby to Clipston and Harborough. But the road to Clipston probably did not exist in 1645. A very clear and detailed map of Naseby made in 1630 [1] shows only one lane running north-east from Naseby, the one to Kelmarsh, while only the most vestigial of tracks led due north towards Sibbertoft. There seems, in fact, to have been no road leading even approximately towards the enemy for the New Model to follow, and the general lie of the ground suggests the probability (no more) that it was moving forward on a line to the left of the modern Naseby–Clipston road. But 'yonder hill', which it now occupied on Cromwell's suggestion, was evidently the ridge on which it eventually fought, [2] though

1. Ipswich and East Suffolk Record Office, *Fitzgerald Collection* (*Acc. 2803*). I owe my knowledge of this map to Mr J. W. S. Mansell, the present vicar of Naseby.

2. This is the clear sense of Sir Henry Slingsby in his Memoirs, and of 'W.G.' whose *A Just Apology for an Abused Army* (1647) records the conversation between Cromwell and Fairfax. The late Colonel A. H. Burne's picture, in his *Battlefields of England* (and also in *The Great Civil War*), of the New Model executing a flank march of a whole mile to the left after it had formed up for battle seems to me a straining of the evidence; and as a hypothesis it becomes unnecessary once one gets rid of the Clipston road.

its first position on it was probably not quite the same as the one it finally adopted.

Rupert, seeing this backward movement of Cromwell's cavalry, either surmised (as one or two contemporaries state) that the New Model had decided not to fight at all, or else he simply saw a chance of falling on it before it was ready to receive him. At any rate, he sent for the rest of the army to come up as quickly as possible, and rode on to seek the best ground on which to draw it up. Straight ahead of him – he was probably a little forward of Clipston – the ground looked marshy and treacherous. It still is after heavy rain. But there seemed a better approach to the enemy by the slope which rose to his right, and he set off to reconnoitre it. On Dust Hill he found what he wanted: a gentle slope leading down to the open expanse called Broad Moor, which rose again on the other side a little higher, but still quite gently, to the westward end of the ridge on which the New Model was deploying. Soon the royal army, with the King in full armour at its head, was marching as fast as it could to join him, retaining as far as possible the order of battle in which it had already formed up.

Few of Fairfax's men saw much of it until it burst in all its gallantry of floating colours and glinting arms and armour upon the ridge facing them, less than a mile away. It was marching westward across their front, to take up a position well to the left of what they expected. This however they interpreted as an attempt to gain the advantage of the wind, which was blowing briskly from the north-west, for in those days before smoke-less powder no army cared to fight with the acrid cloud from musket and cannon-fire blowing back in its soldiers' faces. To avoid this, and also the danger of being outflanked, they conformed to the royalists' movements, bringing their left flank almost up to Sulby hedges and forming their front to face due north. Their front indeed now filled the whole width, nearly a mile in extent, of Naseby Field, whose eastern boundary ran two or three hundred yards to the right of the present

Sibbertoft road.[1] The field lay fallow that summer, though some patches of corn grew on the royalists' slope opposite. Open though it was, however, it was broken by swampy patches and unexpected ditches, while the bottom of Broad Moor was full of furze bushes and a large rabbit warren lay before the parliamentarian right.

Just before he finally ordered his forces, Fairfax took the unusual step of drawing his whole front back about a hundred paces, so that most of it was hidden from the royalists behind the brow of the ridge. Its commanders, of course, riding before their regiments, could watch the enemy's movements sufficiently. Skippon did not like this move much, but he could not get the order rescinded, so like the good soldier he was he got on with the job of marshalling the infantry. Secrecy does not seem to have been Fairfax's object, for like the royalists he disposed his forces conventionally with the infantry in the centre and his cavalry on either wing. But he may have been concerned to put as little strain as possible upon the morale of his greener troops, and to avoid encouraging the enemy by any signs of confusion among them. At least he spared them the strain of watching, massed in the open without any kind of cover, while an embattled army advanced steadily to the charge in a forest of cold steel. If doubts of his infantry's steadfastness were his motive, the events of the day were to justify him.

The ordering of the cavalry fell naturally to Cromwell, and he was later to recall poignantly the sudden uplift of spirit which came upon him as he went about it. 'I could not,' he wrote, 'riding alone about my business, but smile out to God in praises, in assurance of victory, because God would, by things that are not, bring to naught things that are. Of which I

1. J. Sprigge (*Anglia Rediviva*, p. 40) states that the armies where they fought exactly filled the whole extent of the field, and the 1630 map establishes where its boundaries ran. One reason why Colonel Burne's reconstruction of the eastern side of the battle differs from mine is that he places both armies about 500 yards further east. If my siting of them is correct, the actual lie of the ground makes it likelier that Cromwell posted his right wing slightly forward rather than backward of Skippon's infantry.

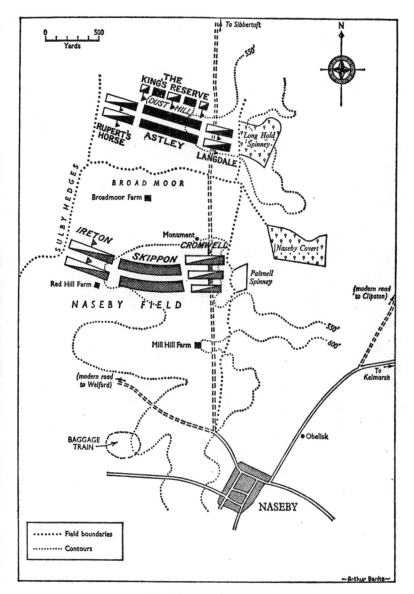

The Battle of Naseby

had great assurance; and God did it.' At the last moment he sought out Colonel John Okey of the dragoons, that burly, obstinate, great-hearted sectary who as a diehard republican was to be such a thorn in his side in later years. He found Okey in a meadow half a mile back, issuing ammunition to his tired men, who had been on outpost duty every night during the approach march. But dragoons were just what Cromwell needed to line Sulby hedges, which ran forward towards the enemy from the New Model's extreme left flank, for from that position their carbines could both gall Rupert's cavalry as it charged and cover the left wing against a flanking attack. They had barely time to dismount and take up position before they were in action.

For the two armies did not stand long facing each other. Rupert's purpose was to strike as soon as he had his forces ready – sooner, his critics said afterwards. To catch his enemy on one foot was his best hope of making up for his inferiority in numbers, for he brought 9000 men at the most against nearly 14,000. The disparity in infantry was not so great but that quality (on the royalist side) might well tell against quantity, but in cavalry it was crippling. Cromwell, when Colonel Rossiter joined him on the field at the last minute with 400 horse from Lincolnshire, disposed of about 6500 horse, including dragoons. Against all these Rupert could oppose perhaps 4500, and he must have thought bitterly of Goring's seasoned troopers, far away in Somerset. They indeed might have given the day a different outcome; more than any other one factor, Goring's disobedience spelt the ruin of the last army which Charles I was to lead in the field.

Rupert himself joined his brother Maurice at the head of the cavalry on his right wing. With the King in the field in person to take the commander-in-chief's place in the centre, behind his main infantry 'battle', Rupert had a pretext to ride where he loved best to ride, with his own charging horsemen. His own and Maurice's regiments, with their life guards and the Queen's regiment, made up his first line, and he had two more regiments for a second. Facing the Princes, in command of the parliamentarian left, was Ireton, whom Fairfax had raised only that morning, at Cromwell's request, to the post of Commissary-General or second-in-command of the horse. Slight of build and with an almost feminine delicacy of feature, Ireton was never a brilliant soldier, but he was to justify his promotion as he had earned it, by unremitting zeal, uncommon gifts of organization and a courage which did not need the fever of action or the balm of victory to sustain it. Now thirty-four years old, he was soon to marry Cromwell's daughter Bridget, and to exercise a greater influence on his father-in-law than any other single man. What drew Cromwell to him was Ireton's Puritan faith, no less deeply grounded for being less emotional than his own, and the keen grave mind which was to make him the army's foremost tactician when it turned from fighting to politics. But this day's business was to fight, and Ireton, though his five regiments outnumbered the Princes' in actual strength by three to two, was to find himself outmatched.

Lord Astley, a sixty-six-year-old veteran of the Nether-lands school, commanded the royalist foot in the centre. His first and stronger line was supported by two squadrons of cavalry, and his second by another. Behind that came the King with the reserve: his mounted life guard in the centre, flanked on either side by his own and Rupert's regiments of foot, and these in turn flanked by detachments of the Newark horse. The New Model foot was marshalled more simply, with no interspersing of infantry and cavalry. Skippon had a first line of five regiments and a second of three, with a small re-serve or rearguard behind and a forlorn hope of 300 musketeers well down the slope in front.

The royalist left was composed of Langdale's brigade, in-corporating what remained of Newcastle's horse which had fought at Marston Moor, together with the rest of the Newark horse.[1] Their prospects of success, discontented as they were

1. Brigadier P. Young, in a valuable article on 'The Northern Horse at Naseby' in the *Journal of the Society for Army Historical Research* (1954), establishes that the average strength of Langdale's regiments was under 100.

at the whole course of the campaign and numbering only about 2000, was not improved by a petty quarrel between Langdale and the Newark contingent's commander. Behind the brow of the hill opposite, Cromwell could afford to range his regiments in three lines against Langdale's two. His first was largely composed of the troops of his own famous double regiment of the Eastern Association. Fairfax's regiment on his right and Whalley's on his left had both been formed from it when the New Model was organized, and yet another of its troops had gone into Sir Robert Pye's in the centre. When Rossiter's Lincolnshire horse added themselves to Cromwell's extreme right, he had about 3500 men.

Each army was given a 'field word' as a means of identification in the confusion of battle, 'Queen Mary' for the King's army and 'God our strength' for the New Model. The royalists wore beanstalks as a field sign, and though none was enjoined upon Fairfax's men, some of them agreed among themselves to wear white tokens in their hats, as at Marston Moor.

As Fairfax and Cromwell had all along expected, it was the royalists who advanced to the charge. Scarcely any gunfire preceded the clash of the two armies. Rupert had not waited to bring up more than a few light field pieces, and Fairfax had left all but half a dozen of his guns with his baggage train, well behind his left wing. These forward guns had time to fire only one round as the royalists came on. It was not long past ten o'clock when they moved in brave order over Broad Moor, moving at a smart pace and keeping their formations well. 'Very stately', Okey described their progress from his perilous vantage-point, and Fairfax's forlorn hope had to fall back before them. As they climbed the slope towards the New Model, its whole line moved forward over the brow to gain the advantage of the incline, and for the first time the two armies really saw each other. The clash was almost simultaneous all along the front. But the two Princes' charge, very typically, led the rest by a little, and for clarity's sake we shall follow the crowded events of the next half hour from their end of the battle on the west to Cromwell's and Langdale's on the east.

Rupert and Maurice had not only to charge uphill against superior numbers but to run the gauntlet of Okey's dragoons, whose carbines emptied not a few saddles.[1] But this was Rupert's element, and his crack front line never faltered. As it came up the slope, Ireton led his forward regiments down to meet it, over ground which proved unexpectedly troublesome. First the Princes and then Ireton halted briefly to dress their lines, then they fell on each other. Ireton was at the head of his own regiment on the right of his front line, and in the confused mêlée which now ensued he rode with it clean through the Queen's and Maurice's regiments. But these cavaliers were far from being broken, and in the heat of action Ireton too easily lost control of his wing as a whole. Seeing on his right how hard the royalist foot were pressing Skippon's men, he led his regiment right in among them. It was gallant enough, but disastrous. His horse was shot from under him, a pike ran him through the thigh, a halberd slashed his face, and for a while he was a helpless prisoner. Meanwhile on the left of his line Colonel Butler was wounded and his regiment overcome by the Princes' charge, and when their second line followed them into the attack the whole of the New Model's left wing gave way. Some parts of it, though not all, fled from the field all the way to Northampton – men newly raised from the eastern counties, it was said, and 'better armed than hearted'. Once again Rupert's charge carried all before it, and once again it was carried too far. Rupert did not, or could not, halt his troops till they came to Fairfax's baggage train far behind the lines.

Only moments after the Princes' onslaught came the clash of the two main infantry 'battles' in the centre. When Skippon's men came over the brow to meet Astley's they were within musket-shot of each other, and they exchanged only one volley before they came to push of pike, the musketeers club-

---

1. This proves that the Princes' charge ran close to Sulby hedges, which command only a very limited field of fire. Okey's own narrative indeed suggests that some royalist cavalry charged *west of* the hedge, enveloping his dragoons, but his sense is not very clear.

bing each other lustily with the butts of their weapons. The royalist foot were at the most 4000 against 7000 or more; they had marched hard that morning, with little sleep after their more than twenty-mile trek the day before, and the slope was against them. Yet it was the parliamentarian line which gave. On its right Fairfax's own regiment stood firm enough, but in the centre and still more on the left, it wavered, then fell back. The left-hand regiment was Skippon's, newly formed out of weak units from Essex's and Manchester's armies. Its lieutenant-colonel was killed, and Skippon himself was wounded under the ribs by a musket-ball which pierced and splintered his armour. He managed to keep his horse and refused to leave the field till the battle was over, but discouragement spread swiftly among his soldiers. Far along the line, the ranks were soon in extreme disorder; their colours began to fall, and the men started running back to shelter behind the second line in their rear. Many of their officers, failing in all their efforts to steady them, stood grimly round their colours and retired only far enough to fall in with the second line, which now came on. But whether its three regiments could have stopped the rot is doubtful, had not help come from another quarter.

The whole fortune of the day now hung on the success of Cromwell and the right wing. Cromwell like Ireton led his men down the slope, a steeper one this side, as Langdale came up it. Whalley's regiment on his left was first engaged, for the rest of his line was slowed up by the rabbit warrens and furze-bushes. Whalley's men and Langdale's two right-hand squadrons fired their pistols at almost point-blank range, then fell on each other with their swords. After a brief but fierce struggle the two royalist squadrons broke and fled to shelter behind the King's reserve; but before this the mêlée had become general as Cromwell's and Rossiter's troops moved into action on the right. With their broader front they poured round Langdale's left flank, and sheer numbers told as body after tight-ranked body of them pressed forward into the fight. Langdale's whole wing was soon flying to the rear; its rout was even more complete than Ireton's on the other side of the field. But Cromwell was not going to squander victory in a reckless free-for-all-pursuit. At his command four bodies of his horse (possibly his whole first line) rode off in close, disciplined order after the fleeing northerners, just far enough to ensure that they did not rally and reform; then they drew rein. As they passed close by the King's reserve, Charles made a pathetic attempt to lead a counter-attack. He was actually about to charge them at the head of his horse guards when the Scottish Earl of Carnwath, riding next to him, seized his bridle, cried with an oath, 'Will you go upon your death?' and pulled the royal charger round away from the enemy. Word then passed along the bewildered ranks behind to march to the right, which (since the pursuing cavalry were obviously on the left) they took to mean that they were to save themselves as best they could. They galloped away in disorder for a quarter of a mile before they could be halted and partially rallied.

Cromwell, having kept the main body of his cavalry intact, now drew it together for the decisive stroke of the battle. Thanks to his own battle sense and the perfect discipline of his regiments, he was able to make his superiority in numbers tell to the full. The infantry battle on his left had been raging for about half an hour, and the New Model foot, though badly disordered, was not yet broken beyond the possibility of rally-ing. The royalist infantry, on the other hand, close though it must have felt to victory and richly though it had earned it, was now unprotected on both flanks. On its right the Princes' had charged clean off the field, while on the left Langdale had been beaten from it. Even the King's life guard in their rear seemed to have deserted them. Upon their open left flank Cromwell now charged, and their fate was sealed. Fairfax was with him, riding into the midst of the pikes bareheaded, for early on he had lost his helmet in the thick of the fighting. He was transported by the daemon which always took possession of his modest soul on the battlefield, and over this field he ranged freely, encouraging many a regiment by his oblivion to danger and his visible assurance of victory. 'His very coun-tenance discovered an emblem of true valour', wrote one of his officers; he 'had a spirit heightened above the ordinary spirit of man'.

Soon the royalist foot were under attack from other quarters too. Those of Ireton's horse who had not fled the field had made their way round behind their foot to be re-formed into some sort of fighting order not far from Cromwell's initial position, and from there they now joined in the assault. From Sulby hedges on the other side, Okey brought his dragoons into action once more. They had given themselves up for lost when Ireton's wing broke, but they had defended themselves fiercely, and when the Princes' troops swept on southward the tide of battle had passed them by. Now, when he saw Cromwell attacking the opposite flank of the royalist foot, Okey promptly mounted his men and led them like fully-fledged cavalry in a highly successful charge from the west. Pressed on three sides and with no prospect of relief, the royalists began to lay down their arms and ask for quarter. Only one brigade or 'tertia', consisting probably of Rupert's bluecoat regiment and the King's own,[1] called up from their reserve, fought to the last. Twice at least its serried pikes repulsed the pick of the New Model horse, including Fairfax's life guard. Its square was only broken when Fairfax brought up his own foot regiment to club its way in with its musket-butts while his cavalry charged it in both flanks simultaneously. The ensign who carried its colours fell to Fairfax's own sword.

Rupert meanwhile had lost all touch with the battle. It is very hard to rally cavalry after a successful charge, and after breaking Ireton's ranks it may be that Rupert could not have halted his men had he tried. What checked them eventually was the guard on Fairfax's baggage train, nearly a mile behind the battle. At first its commander mistook Rupert, who was wearing a red cap called a montero very like Fairfax's, for his

---

1. I am assuming that Sprigge (p. 38), Whitelocke (*Memorials*, 1682 ed., p. 145), *The Kingdom's Weekly Intelligencer* (10–17 June) and Rushworth's letter in *Thomason Tract E288* (26) all refer to the same action, but the bluecoats' resistance may have been separate from that of the 'tertia' which Fairfax charged.

own General, and he went to him hat in hand to ask how the day went. Rupert brusquely asked him and his men if they would have quarter. He answered with a loud cry of 'no!' and a volley from their flintlocks. Rather than engage in a minor battle for the train while the main one was still in doubt, Rupert took the chance to pull his scattered horsemen together and led them back, none too willing, the way they had come.

One glance at the field on his return must have convinced him of the folly which had led him, as commander-in-chief in all but name, to charge with his leading squadrons. It was too late to go to the help of his infantry, and in any case his dishevelled ranks were in no state to take on the ordered and disciplined bodies of horse that Cromwell still disposed of. So he made his way round, closely followed by some bodies of Ireton's horse which had re-formed, to where the King with his life guard was trying to rally what was left of Langdale's shaken cavalry, somewhat beyond the bottom of Broad Moor. There they were faced, but not yet engaged, by those regiments of Cromwell's which had pursued them after the initial charge. A lull had fallen, for word was sent to these regiments not to attack until the foot could be brought down to support them. Fairfax, who need take no chances now, was evidently determined that the final stroke should be overwhelming. His infantry was a quarter of a mile back, still mopping the royalist foot and taking prisoners by the hundred, but now it was swiftly brought into line and marched down to within carbine shot of the King's horse. Amid a silence which contrasted strangely with the din of battle a little earlier, the New Model was formed up afresh, 'a second good battalia at the latter end of the day', with its infantry in the centre and cavalry once more on either flank. The King had no infantry left, and neither Langdale's nor Rupert's troopers could be brought to a second charge. The ominous quiet was broken by a volley from Okey's dragoons, in preparation for the final assault. It was never delivered. The hastily-drawn royalist ranks melted and fled from the field rather than face it, though Rupert and Charles risked their lives trying to make them stand.

This time the pursuit was immediate and thorough. Cromwell's troopers – much to their displeasure, as they thought of the spoils of Leicester clinking in the enemy's pockets and piled on his wagons – were ordered not to dismount for plunder on pain of death. They obeyed, and their swords did heavy execution all along the road to Leicester as far as Great Glen, where the Earl of Lichfield, commander of the King's life guard, finally managed to organize a stand against them. Sir Henry Slingsby recorded a vivid glimpse of fleeing soldiers risking death a second time to pick up the money spilt on the ground from overturned wagons in the leaguer behind the royalist lines. In this same leaguer, when the victorious infantry came up to it, a more horrible slaughter took place. Hundreds of terrified women who had followed the King's army were huddled there, most of them what the royalist soldiers called 'leaguer bitches' of the kind that has followed armies from time immemorial, though others were soldiers' wives. Many of these spoke no English and were taken for Irish, though Miss Wedgwood has suggested[1] it is much likelier that they were the wives of some of the many Welshmen in the King's army. Their captors slew at least a hundred of these poor souls out of hand, and marked most of the rest of the women as whores in the brutal manner of the time by slashing their faces or slitting their noses. There is no palliating this outrage, which at least ten London news-sheets reported without a hint of shame or apology. It can only be said that it seems to have been perpetrated by the as yet ill-disciplined infantry, not by Cromwell's veteran cavalry which was fully engaged in the pursuit. A report had been current in the New Model's quarters a week before the battle that a thousand Irishwomen followed the King's camp, in addition to the cavaliers' English drabs,[2] and Parliament itself had done all it could to spread the view that all the Irish were sub-human monsters whose hands dripped with the blood of innocent Protestants.

The King got safely through to Leicester, where he paused

1. C. V. Wedgwood, *The King's War*, p. 455.
2. *Perfect Occurrences*, 6–13 June.

just long enough for the two Princes to join him, and to give orders for the care of the wounded and reorganization of the garrison. Though he had left the field twenty miles behind him, he did not feel safe until he had ridden another seventeen that evening to Ashby-de-la-Zouch. He had lost his entire infantry, and only the remnants of Rupert's and Langdale's horse were with him now. The actual slaughter had not been very great though the cavalry had as usual suffered at least as heavily in the pursuit as on the field. The more trustworthy estimates of the royalist dead range between 400 and 1000, against no more than 150 of the New Model. But quarter had been readily granted to the King's infantry, and altogether Fairfax had fully 4500 prisoners on his hands. Most of them, except for the wounded who were taken to Northampton, were crammed into the church at Market Harborough that night then marched by easy stages to London to be paraded through the City streets in a kind of Roman triumph. Among the fifty-six colours exhibited there was a cavalry standard of green flowered damask, with the inscription 'cuckolds we come' surmounted by a pair of horns. (Its captors had turned it joyously against the royalists in their next charge.) Among the more solid prizes were all the King's guns, several thousand arms, much powder and ammunition, a welcome store of biscuit and cheese (for Fairfax's men had fought on empty stomachs) – in fact the entire baggage train, including the coaches and sumpter-wagons of the King, Rupert and other chief commanders. Although the best of the loot from Leicester had been carted away to Newark, enough remained in the wagons and the prisoners' purses to offer rich booty to the victorious army. But the capture which did the King most hurt was that of all his correspondence, including copies of the letters that had passed between him and the Queen in the last two years. They exposed to shocked eyes at Westminster his protracted efforts to bring over an army of Irish papists, and his readiness in return to abolish the penal laws against the Catholics in England. This seemed almost worse than his plans to hire 10,000 foreign mercenaries under the Duke of Lorraine, and his attempt to get money or men or both from the Kings of France and Denmark and the Prince of Orange. Naturally the Parliament published these letters. War was war, and it was well that supporters of the peace party should know what kind of a man they would have to deal with. Naturally, too, *The King's Cabinet Opened* created a sensation when it appeared on the bookstalls. One wonders whether it did Charles more harm among his enemies or his would-be friends.

There were still many on the parliamentary side, however, who would never admit themselves to be the King's enemies, and the news of the New Model's victory did not bring them unmixed joy. The Presbyterians had even half hoped that this creature of their political opponents would discredit itself, for its victory was the victory of men who would have no peace with the King save on terms of surrender. The purity of the gospel also seemed in danger; this the Scots felt especially. There was little reassurance in the fact that Fairfax and many other officers were not extremists, either in religion or politics. It was feared, and not without reason, that the New Model would take its spiritual cue from Cromwell, and from such of its colonels as Rainsborough, Rich, Fleetwood, Okey and Pride. Late in the evening after the battle, weary after many long hours in the saddle, Cromwell wrote his own brief dispatch to the Speaker. He ended it with a warm tribute to Fairfax and a plea, one of many that were to come from his pen or voice, for liberty of conscience for all who had fought with him:

> Honest men served you faithfully in this action. Sir, they are trusty; I beseech you in the name of God not to discourage them. I wish this action may beget thankfulness and humility in all that are concerned in it. He that ventures his life for the liberty of his country, I wish he trust God for the liberty of his conscience, and you for the liberty he fights for.

It was typical of the Commons that in publishing his letter they deleted this last paragraph. (Another pamphlet, authorized in a fit of inattention by the Lords, let the cat out of the bag by printing the whole text.) But as a soldier Cromwell had shown himself more than ever indispensable, and at the first oportunity the Commons voted to continue him as Lieutenant-General during the pleasure of the two Houses. The Lords, however, who had so far not confirmed his appointment at all, now agreed to do so only for a term of three months.

At Naseby, the King lost his chance of outweighing his enemies' mounting advantage in material resources with superior military skill. He was never again to collect an army capable of meeting the New Model in the field. It was no dishonour for 9000 men to have been beaten, and not easily beaten, by nearly 14,000, but it must have been agonizing to recollect impotently the errors which had forced them to fight against such odds. Of these, Goring's bland refusal to come to his master's help stood high above the rest, for with his 3000 horse on the left wing the battle could have gone very differently. But there was much else for reproach, besides this lamentable defection: those six days of loitering at Daventry, all the inconsistency of purpose brought about by personal antagonisms in the King's council of war, the foolish contempt for the New Model and its General, and Charles's readiness to listen to Digby and Ashburnham rather than his own commander-in-chief. The gravest military weakness, however, was the failure of intelligence which caused so much groping during the campaign as a whole, and allowed the royal army to be surprised on two successive days just before the battle. The other side had the benefit of Brereton's prompt and accurate reports of the royalists' movements from Market Drayton to Leicester, and of Luke's remarkably efficient intelligence service between Leicester and Naseby. It greatly helped the New Model, of course, that it was operating in territory where a number of friendly garrisons could keep watch for it, but even so the contrast in efficiency between the Scoutmaster-Generals of the two sides is striking. And in the final hasty marshalling of his forces on Dust Hill, had Rupert any idea of the strength of Cromwell's right wing when he pitted the

northern horse against it? Would he, with fuller knowledge of
the enemy's dispositions, still have taken that rash decision to
charge with his right wing, thereby abdicating such control as
he might have exercised over the course of the battle through
the employment of the King's reserve?

As for the New Model's victory, it owed as much to Cromwell's cavalry as had that of the allied armies at Marston Moor,
and it is worth remarking again how many of the troops on that
crucial right wing of his were those he had personally trained.
Naseby was certainly not won by the invincible qualities of the
new army as a whole. It had after all only just been formed,
largely from reluctant conscripts and the disgruntled remnants
of older and less happy armies. It had been forced to take the
field prematurely, and had since then been misemployed in a
manner which might have damped the spirits of a much better-
knit force. In the event it behaved neither better nor worse than
might have been expected. But Naseby was a turning-point, the
great beginning of a course of victories which was to give its
soldiers faith in their officers, their General and their cause,
and shape them into a single, superb fighting instrument.

Two days after the battle, the famous divine Richard Baxter
visited the army and witnessed with dismay the wildfire of
sectarian enthusiasm spreading through its ranks. Though he
stayed to labour among the soldiers as a chaplain, all his efforts
to contain their speculations within the bounds of moderate
Puritan orthodoxy were in vain. Out of the ferment of preaching and the heat of battle would soon be forged a genuine
revolutionary spirit, radical in politics as in religion, and poles
apart in its vision of a New Jerusalem from the limited, lawyer-
bound objectives which the Long Parliament had first set itself. Naseby gave this army, in its corporate existence, its
baptism of fire; Preston was to lay England at its feet. Between
the two battles the English Revolution advanced to its climax.

7

Victory Without Peace

A WEEK AFTER Naseby Charles was at Hereford, and almost as sanguine as ever. Leicester had fallen to the New Model, but he had salvaged about 4000 horse, and Gerrard had at last brought in his Welsh levies to give him the nucleus of a new infantry. He could still hope that Goring would capture Taunton at last and bring the western army to join his own, and he pursued his Irish schemes more urgently and recklessly than ever. But Fairfax gave him no respite. As soon as Leicester surrendered he marched straight after Goring, while Leven's Scots, strengthened somewhat when Carlisle finally fell to them on 28 June, moved south more slowly to undertake the siege of Hereford. Goring was brought to battle at Langport on 10 July. Fairfax and Cromwell staked success on a cavalry charge through a lane only a few yards wide, and it came off; six troops of horse and a few picked companies of musketeers caused the rout of Goring's whole army, half of which was captured or killed. Less than a fortnight later the last hope of a royalist stand in the west died when Fairfax took Bridgwater, and Rupert could only advise the King to treat for peace. All that was best in Charles showed in his reply:

> If I had any other quarrel but the defence of my religion, crown and friends, you had full reason for your advice. For I confess that, speaking either as to mere soldier or statesman, I must say there is no probability but of my ruin. But as to Christian, I must tell you that God will not suffer rebels to prosper, or His cause to be overthrown; and whatever personal punishment it shall please Him to inflict upon me must not make me repine, much less to give over this quarrel. . . . Though I must avow to all my friends, that he that will stay with me at this time must expect and resolve either to die for a good cause, or, which is worse, to live as miserable in the

maintaining it as the violence of insulting rebels can make him.

So Charles marched from Cardiff northward through Wales – only to be threatened in his rear by a crushing defeat of the Pembrokeshire royalists early in August; then from Ludlow north-east to Doncaster – only to be threatened by the approach of Leslie's Scottish horse and the Yorkshire forces, now under Major-General Poyntz. What had drawn him north was news of another victory by Montrose at Alford; but before he could know that his champion had won yet another, still more brilliant, at Kilsyth on 15 August, he was forced to retreat, and by the 28th he was back in Oxford. Two days later he was marching westward again, to try to save Hereford. There he received the bitterest news of all, when Rupert surrendered Bristol to Fairfax on 11 September. Rupert had told Charles he could hold the city for four months, but he had reckoned too lightly the crippling odds against him in numbers, the disaffection of the citizens and the blazing fury with which the New Model, already transformed since Naseby, threw itself into the assault. Charles, his judgement corroded by Digby's bitter insinuations, conceived he was betrayed. Without a hearing he dismissed his nephew from all his commands and offices, and sent him a pass so that he might leave the kingdom at once. This last unkindest cut was spared, however; there was a partial reconciliation in the autumn, and Rupert did not have to leave England until Parliament ordered him to do so after Oxford had surrendered. But it was a tragic outcome to three years of devoted and sometimes brilliant service, and it added another brave name to the long roll-call of the wronged servants of the Stuarts.

We must pass briefly over the last sad stages of the war. A second attempt by Charles to join Montrose by way of Lancashire was wrecked when Poyntz routed the royal cavalry under Langdale at Rowton Heath near Chester on 24 September. Charles did not yet know that eleven days earlier Montrose's bright chain of victories had been broken at Philiphaugh by a defeat so entire that he never recovered sufficiently to fight again. That autumn all south Wales and Monmouthshire were lost, while famous royalist garrisons fell one by one in the west, the south and the midlands, and Leven and Poyntz formed the siege of Newark. The early months of 1646 saw Fairfax wrest Devon and Cornwall from Hopton, and in February Chester fell at last to Brereton. Hopton had to surrender next month, and the last royalist force left in the field was beaten at Stow-on-the-Wold. The final operation was the siege of Oxford, whose capitulation in June brought the first Civil War virtually to an end.

Long before that, both sides had been manœuvring for advantage in the coming tussle over peace terms. Charles had quickly seen his chance of playing off the Independents against the Presbyterians, and the Scots against both. The Scots indeed were so resentful of their treatment by the English, and so distrustful of the Independents' and the New Model's intentions towards their King, that they were drawn into negotiations for restoring him long before the fighting ended. A French agent acted as intermediary, and right-wing English Presbyterians like Holles were in the intrigue too. But this did not prevent Charles from making overtures to the Independents as well. From the tangle of secret diplomacy in the war's last autumn and winter, two facts stand out. One is that between the Scots' insistence on Presbyterianism throughout Britain and Charles's unyielding adherence to the Church of England, there was no room for honest compromise. The other is that Charles was spoiling his chance of winning the support of Scottish and English Presbyterians by the way he was bidding for a very different kind of assistance elsewhere. Approaches to the Prince of Orange, the King of Denmark and the French clergy; a ruinous treaty signed with the confederate Irish; a mission to Rome by Sir Kenelm Digby to seek papal contributions towards the upkeep of the expected Irish army – these were among the revelations which shocked Parliament during the war's later stages, and played into the war party's hands.

Faced in March and April 1646 with the appalling prospect of capture, Charles boldly requested permission of the Parliament to return to Westminster. When the Houses refused to receive him without his first giving satisfaction for the past and security for the future, he tried to open negotiations with the army leaders, but they would have nothing to do with him behind the Parliament's back. So late in April he slipped out of Oxford through the besiegers' lines and made his way incognito to the Scots' camp before Newark. There he ordered his garrison to surrender, and the Scots marched off with him to Newcastle. There was great consternation at Westminster, for possession of the King's person could be a trump card in the impending diplomatic struggle – if indeed it remained merely diplomatic. But Charles found himself a prisoner. No formula could be found whereby the Scots would help him recover his throne without forcing his conscience over the Church. They might let him off taking the Covenant personally, but they insisted on his agreeing to the establishment of Presbyterianism in England. The Queen and such courtiers as Digby and Ashburnham urged him to give way, but, tricky as his dealings were with the Scots on many points (and theirs with him), he would not deceive them on this one.

Charles's refusal to sacrifice his Church lost him for a time the support of the Scots and the chance to split the English Parliament. After months of debate the two Houses agreed on the peace terms they would put to him, and Argyle, who was still the master of Scotland, came to London in June 1646 to approve them. By these Propositions of Newcastle, as they were called, Charles was to take the Covenant, impose it on all his subjects and confirm the Presbyterian national church which Parliament was busy establishing. Parliament was to control the armed forces for the next twenty years. More than sixty of the King's chief supporters were to expect no pardon, and all other royalists of any substance were to lose varying proportions of their estates, according to their 'delinquency'. Charles would do nothing so final as to reject these terms outright, but he could never accept them. The Scottish Parliament decided in December, however, that unless he did accept them it could not receive him as King of Scotland. A week later,

Scots and English finally agreed over the bill to be settled for the Scottish army's services in the war. In January 1647, when the first instalment was paid, the Scots departed homewards from Newcastle and handed Charles over to the English Parliament's commissioners. It was easy, though unjust, for royalists to accuse them of selling their King.

As Charles was escorted southward to his new captivity at Holmby House in Northamptonshire, the church bells rang in his honour and in town after town the people turned out to demonstrate their affection. Fairfax was among those who rode to greet him and kiss his hand. None but a few extremists yet dreamed of a settlement which would not centre on the person of Charles as King. And Charles had already begun to soften up the sticklers at Westminster with clever counter-offers: ten years' parliamentary control of the forces instead of twenty, and a three years' trial for Presbyterianism, for instance. (Three years of royalist reaction would have made the Anglican Church safe enough.) There was little hope of genuine agreement, but Charles was not so much seeking reconciliation as parrying his conquerors' demands until they fell out among themselves. He was playing his hand shrewdly now, and they fell out sooner, perhaps, than he had dared to hope.

Once the Scots had gone home and left the King in English hands, there was less need for a large army in England. The balance at Westminster swung from the Independents, the New Model's creators and allies, to the Presbyterians, who on political and religious grounds thoroughly distrusted it. Many local forces had already been disbanded, and it was reasonable that the New Model should at least be reduced. The country was war-weary, trade was hard hit and taxation high, and the first of a series of bad harvests had made food dear. If only the Presbyterians could have treated the army with bare justice and a little tact, they would have had the co-operation of its commanders and the overwhelming support of public opinion in reducing it. But between February and April they set about it with such provocation to its officers and such a shabby disregard for the soldiers' just claims that they ended by uniting all ranks against them. Disbandment was not at first such a grievance in itself, for the expeditionary force which was planned for Ireland and the many garrisons still needed at home would provide employment for most of those who really wanted to go on soldiering. But by threatening the army's cherished liberty of conscience and discriminating against its Independent officers, the Presbyterians needlessly antagonized it. But what really angered the soldiers most was that their pay was eighteen weeks in arrears in the infantry and forty-three weeks in the cavalry, and there was no assurance that they would get it.

Not unnaturally the officers, especially the strong Independents among them, showed signs of questioning the terms under which they were expected to serve in Ireland, but they got no encouragement in resistance from their generals. Cromwell had recently undertaken to the Commons that the army would disband whenever it was ordered to. What touched off the explosion was a spontaneous petition from the soldiers. Though they only voiced their own legitimate grievances, and were persuaded by their officers to address themselves to Fairfax and not to Parliament, the two Houses were so incensed that without investigating the facts they passed a declaration, penned by Holles, 'that all those who shall continue in their distempered condition, and go on advancing and promoting that petition, shall be looked upon and proceeded against as enemies of the state and disturbers of the public peace'. The words bit deep into the soldiers' minds. Whose enemies were they, who had borne the heat of battle in the Parliament's cause? The last straw came at the end of April, when they were voted a mere six weeks' pay. No wonder that little more than one in ten of the New Model's soldiers volunteered for service in Ireland. During April most of the cavalry regiments spontaneously elected 'Agitators' – the word then signified no more than agents – to represent their grievances, and next month the rest of the army, infantry included, followed suit. Meanwhile Cromwell, like Fairfax, was still striving to keep them in obedience to the Parliament's authority.

But the Parliament pressed them too far. Resolving on immediate disbandment, to begin on 1 June, it ordered the regiments
to several widely separated rendezvous, to prevent trouble.
Scotland had sent commissioners to London again, and the
Presbyterian leaders were discussing plans with them for bringing the Scottish army back into England with the Prince of
Wales at its head, if it should be needed. They hoped it would
not. Once they brought the King to London, as they now
intended, they could rely on the City militia, 18,000 strong
and officered entirely by Presbyterians, to prevent the army
from interfering. So they reckoned. But the officers' anger at
the betrayal of their cause, and the soldiers' at Parliament's
contempt for their services and their rights, had knit the army
into one. Fairfax's council of war, strongly pressed by the rank
and file, ordered a general rendezvous of all the regiments at
Newmarket on 3 June. Cromwell commanded Cornet Joyce of
Fairfax's life guard to take a party of horse to Holmby and
see that the King was not removed. Joyce went one better.
Hearing that a Presbyterian force much larger than his own
was marching against him, he removed the King himself, and
with Charles's concurrence headed for Newmarket.

To the Parliament, the fearful happenings of these June days
seemed likely a carefully plotted mutiny, with Cromwell as
its great contriver. There was talk of impeaching and arresting
him, and it was in virtual flight that he now rode from Westminster to join the army. He found it in serious disorder, with
the Agitators threatening take over control from its officers.
The way he and Fairfax brought it back to unity and discipline
was by creating a General Council of the Army as a kind of
safety-valve. In this body two officers and two Agitators from
each regiment sat with the generals to debate the soldiers'
grievances and aims, though actual military authority was kept
firmly in the hands of Fairfax's council of war. The whole
army now banded together in a kind of military covenant,
declaring that it would not divide or disband until its General
Council received satisfaction; and satisfaction would have to

include the removal of the Presbyterian leaders who had traduced it to the Parliament.

Before these threats, Parliament and City wavered between appeasement and defiance. When the army again refused to disband and began to advance southward, they attempted to raise a counter-force in London from the trained bands and the old soldiers of the pre-1645 armies. But there was no resisting the New Model in its present mood. From St Albans it published a manifesto which marked a momentous new phase in the revolution. It was no longer merely concerned for its own wrongs; it ventured

> to propound and plead for some provision for our and the kingdom's satisfaction and future security. . . . Especially considering that we were not a mere mercenary army, hired to serve any arbitrary power of a state, but called forth and conjured by the several declarations of Parliament to the defence of our own and the people's just rights and liberties.

Parliament was asked to purge itself of members who were unfit for their trust, fix a date for its own dissolution, and make the next and all future Parliaments more truly representative of the people by completely redistributing the seats on a rational basis and providing for general elections at three-year intervals. As for the King, he must first assent to these reforms, and then his own rights would be settled 'so far as may consist with the right and freedom of the subject'.

This powerful document was the work of Ireton, now the guiding intellect of the army's counsels. The men who acclaimed it were demanding to be heard not just as soldiers but as citizens – and not even as citizens only, but as the spearhead of a people specially blessed by God whose victories, like those of an earlier chosen people, portended some tremendous divine purpose. They felt they were on the side of history, for 'what are all our histories', Cromwell later asked, 'but God manifesting himself that He hath shaken and tumbled down and trampled upon everything that He hath not planted?' Revolutions have a manner of passing out of the control of the moderate constitutionalists who inaugurate them. The process was more belated and less drastic in the England of 1647 than in the France of 1792 or the Russia of October 1917, but it is comparable.

The army was not the only body to put pressure upon the Parliament. London was a stronghold of Presbyterianism, both religious and political, and feeling against the army ran high there. On 26 July a great mob marched to Westminster, besieged the Commons for six hours and finally poured into the House itself, forcing the helpless members to vote for bringing the King immediately to London. Upon this the Speakers of both Houses, with the principal Independent peers and MPs, sought refuge with the army; and on 6 August the army marched into the capital to see them safely back to their places. But this resolved nothing. Even though some of the Presbyterian leaders had now fled overseas, the right-wingers would reassert themselves as soon as the shadow of military force was lifted. Already the General Council of the Army was pressing for a purge of both Houses, and would have carried it out had not Fairfax vetoed it. Parliament, alternately intimidated by citizens and soldiers and split by the King's clever temporizing, seemed in a fair way to losing the peace.

During July the chief officers tried their own hand at negotiating with Charles. Cromwell and Ireton would give away nothing essential that they had fought for, but they still believed like Fairfax that property and the social order would be safest under monarchy. And they still felt morally bound by their pledges to preserve the King's person and rights. The terms they now put to him differed from the Parliament's in proposing co-existence for Anglican and Puritan churches in mutual tolerance, greater lenience towards the beaten royalists and some positive and far-reaching political, social and legal reforms. Charles welcomed them, but only as a further opportunity for playing off his enemies against each other. Ireton put it bluntly to him. 'Sir,' he said, 'you have an intention to be the arbitrator between the Parliament and us, and we mean to be it between your Majesty and the Parliament.'

Ireton was the more exasperated because the very attempt to treat with Charles was landing the generals in trouble with their own men. Since the spring the army had been increasingly penetrated by the doctrines of a body of men called Levellers. They had risen and flourished amidst the *petite bourgeoisie* of the City; now, with a party organization and a busy press at their disposal, the Levellers set out to gain the army and make it their instrument for revolutionary action. Their leader and hero was John Lilburne, whom Manchester had scolded for venturing against Tickhill,[1] and who for his subsequent attacks on Manchester had been imprisoned by the Lords in the Tower. The army was a rich seeding-ground for his ideas. To minds convinced of the equality of all God's saints and already astir with heady prophecies of the destruction of carnal pomp and power, the Levellers offered a concrete programme. All men, they taught, were born with certain equal and indefeasible natural rights; lordship was of man's making, not God's. The people were sovereign, and all free men should join, every two years at least, in electing their representatives to Parliament. All must be equal before the law, and justice should be done in local courts by popularly elected magistrates. Social and economic privilege of every kind must be abolished. The Levellers, in fact, preached radical, primitive democracy, which they believed to have actually existed in England before the Norman conquest. Baxter heard the soldiers ask each other 'What were the Lords of England but William the Conqueror's colonels, or the barons but his majors, or the knights but his captains?' Just as surely as Pym had launched political revolution in '41, the Levellers portended social revolution in '47.

These Leveller influences not only increased the Presbyterians' distrust of the army tenfold, they threatened its whole discipline. Five regiments elected new Agitators in October, all strident mouthpieces of the Leveller line. They demanded that the army should set a term to the present Parliament's sitting, and if it failed them, impose a democratic republic by direct action. They bitterly attacked the generals for trafficking

1. Above, p. 82.

with the King. 'Ye have men amongst you as fit to govern as others to be removed', the Leveller press told the soldiers; 'with a word ye can create new officers. The safety of the people is above all law.' For days on end Cromwell and Ireton wrestled with their spokesman in the General Council of the Army, sitting in Putney Church, and so far as votes went they were worsted. Then Cromwell somehow reasserted his authority and dismissed the Agitators to their units. This did not prevent two regiments from mutinying in mid-November. Cromwell rode at the mutineers with drawn sword as if he would cow them singlehanded – as he almost did. Fewer soldiers were disaffected than the loud mutinous talk had made out, and when they were forced to choose between their old commanders and the new Agitators they rallied to Fairfax and Cromwell. But it had been a red light to the generals (in more senses than one), and it was fine ammunition for the army's enemies.

The effect on the Presbyterians was to double their anxiety to come to terms with the King. A royalist reaction seemed to them a lesser evil now than the dreadful subversion of society which the army's vocal minority threatened, and in this they had a growing weight of popular opinion on their side. The Independents were split. Few wanted to see the old social and political order overturned; Vane and St John, like Cromwell and Ireton, still wanted to treat with Charles on reasonable terms. But a republican left wing was developing under such men as Henry Marten and Colonel Rainsborough, and towards Cromwell Marten was now more bitter than the Presbyterians.

Scotland too was deeply disturbed at the army's irruption into politics. In June Argyle actually offered Charles a Scottish army, but he changed his mind when the King persisted in refusing the Covenant. The Scottish nobles and lairds, however, were so indignant and alarmed at what was happening in England that Argyle's power waned now before that of his rivals, the party led by the Duke of Hamilton and his brother the Earl of Lanark. The Hamiltons were trimmers; though a long way from the royalism of (say) Montrose, they were prepared to do business with Charles without insisting too strongly on the Covenant or on his establishing Presbyterianism in England. They caused two fresh commissioners to be sent to England, Lanark himself and the Chancellor Loudoun. These two joined the Earl of Lauderdale, who was already there, and between mid-October and the end of the year the three of them conducted the fatal negotiation with the King which led to the second Civil War.

On 11 November Charles escaped from Hampton Court, where he had been kept since August, to Carisbrooke Castle on the Isle of Wight. He wanted firstly to free himself from the army's surveillance so that he could treat more freely with the Scots, whom he warmly welcomed, and secondly to secure an easy spring-board for an escape overseas. He was advised that Colonel Hammond, the Governor of Carisbrooke, was a secret sympathiser with his cause. But though Hammond found his position agonizing, his loyalty as a soldier and a parliamentarian won, and Charles found he had escaped one captivity for another. However, he could bargain with the Scots now in comparative secrecy, while from mid-November onwards he kept the Parliament in play with offers of his own more tempting than any he had made hitherto. Cromwell and the officers grew very cold towards him after his escape, but they seemed to matter less now. On 26 December Charles and the three Scots signed a treaty – 'the Engagement', it was called – and buried it, wrapped in lead, in the garden at Carisbrooke. Presbyterianism was to be confirmed in England for a mere three years, and the Independents and all the sects were to be rigorously suppressed. The Covenant was to be confirmed by the Parliaments of both kingdoms, but not forced on those who objected to it. Scotland bound herself, if the Long Parliament should refuse a general disbandment of all forces and a personal treaty with the King in London, to send an army into England to restore him to very nearly his pre-war authority – at England's expense, of course. Two days later Charles turned down the Parliament's last offers. He had committed himself to the Scottish-Presbyterian alliance which, revived by his son in 1650, was for the next three years to discredit his cause and shed much English and Scottish blood in vain. It was an abandonment of negotiation for war and a bid for restoration by conquest – foreign conquest at that, in the eyes of most Englishmen. It gambled on England's internal divisions proving too strong for her national pride, and it aimed at a royalist reaction which would have been as unpropitious for the passionate religious principles of the Scottish nation as for the political progress of the English. It failed inevitably to create any real common cause either between Scots and cavaliers or between cavaliers and English Presbyterians.

Fairfax presiding over the Council of the Army, 1647
From a woodcut in a contemporary pamphlet

At first the King's popularity was not affected. During the winter and spring the greatest moral threat to the army lay in its isolation, and in the rising tide of popular royalist feeling, especially in the City. This extended to the handful of peers who still sat in the Lords. The Commons however took a sterner view of Charles's duplicity, and on 3 January 1648 passed the Vote of No Addresses, declaring they would make no more overtures to him and receive none from him. The Lords reluctantly concurred twelve days later. The Committee of Both Kingsdoms was dissolved and its authority vested in its English members only, strengthened by three more Independents. This Committee of Derby House, as it was called from where it sat, made vigorous preparations against the renewal of war. The army too closed its ranks. Charles himself had removed the main bone of contention within it, by convincing the generals that he was not to be treated with. Many differences remained between them and the Levellers as to how England should be ruled in an ideal future, but this was not the time to pursue them. The mutineers of November were pardoned, and the General Council of the Army quietly broke up as the regiments dispersed to counter the threats of the common enemy. For a series of royalist risings was an essential part of Charles's and Hamilton's plans, and the Scots commissioners lingered in London through January to concert them. On their departure the stage was set for the second Civil War.

8

Preston

TO THE MORE conservative parliamentarians of the first
Civil War, the second offered only a choice of evils. They
wanted the King back, but they knew that if they helped the
cavaliers and the Scots to victory they could say goodbye to
all they had contended for since 1641. On the other hand they
feared that another triumph by the army would bring property,
privilege and Presbytery crashing down before a fury of blas-
phemous, anarchical levelling. A few right-wing Presbyterians
fought for the King; most maintained an unhappy neutrality.
In Parliament, a reliable majority of the Commons recognized,
when all efforts to avert war had failed, that the first task was
to win it. The Lords were far less certain which side they were
on. The City too, like most of the gentry of England now, was
so anxious to see the King on his throne again, and the army
disbanded, that it was less inclined to count the cost than the
parliament-men who knew Charles's evasions and intrigues at
first hand.

Parliament therefore was under constant pressure to come
to terms with the King, if possible before the cavaliers and the
Scots could plunge the country into war again. That it could
not do, for he had rejected its last offers and deliberately
appealed once more to arms. Nevertheless Parliament and
army were fighting the war with different objectives. The Commons were firm in resisting a restoration dictated by royalist
insurgents and Scottish invaders, but that did not mean that
they would not reinstate Charles when a second defeat (they
hoped) had brought him to more reasonable terms. The army
however was setting its heart against reinstating him on any
terms at all. Fairfax wished him no ill, but in political matters
Fairfax was a cipher compared with Cromwell. And Cromwell was walking a tight-rope, distrusted alike by the Presby-

terians, by Marten's republican clique and by many of his own soldiers. Conservative men saw him as the arch-leveller, the dangerous revolutionary who could and would lay monarchy, peerage, perhaps Parliament itself, in the dust. To Marten he was a potential military dictator. To many of his own rank-and-file, on the other hand, he appeared still a temporizer, compromising with the fallen powers of this world for the sake of his own grandeur. Rumour, probably ill-founded, connected him with more than one eleventh-hour attempt between January and March to avert war by a direct approach to the King. Lilburne publicly accused him of high treason.

The time had come to declare himself, at least to his own forces. Late in April he left Westminster for army head-quarters at Windsor, and dealt firmly with a group of Agitators who had been renewing the old Leveller attacks upon the 'grandees', himself chief among them. Court-martialled, they were lucky to get off with a reprimand. Then for three consecutive days Cromwell, officers and Agitators met together for prayer, to search each others' hearts and seek divine guidance. Cromwell earnestly pressed them to consider whether there were any iniquity on their consciences, as an army or as individuals, which might have caused the Lord to withdraw His presence from them. 'Which we found', wrote Adjutant-General Allen afterwards, 'to be those cursed carnal conferences our own conceited wisdom, our fears and want of faith had prompted us, the year before, to entertain with the King and his party.' On the third day came an urgent call for action; all south Wales was in revolt. So they resolved together:

> That it was the duty of our day, with the forces we had, to go out and fight against these potent enemies . . . and if ever the Lord brought us back again in peace, to call Charles Stuart, that man of blood, to an account for that blood he had shed, and mischief he had done to his utmost, against the Lord's cause and people in these poor nations.

The King, in the eyes of these soldiers, was a war criminal; worse, he had caused his standard to be raised again in defiance of the judgement given by the God of battles in his former defeat. He was warring against the people of the Lord. It was a harsh decision, reached through reasonings remote from those whereby we judge public causes today. But it was not lightly taken, and those who took it could have no assurance of victory but their own faith. They knew where one serious defeat could bring them; they did not know how far the divided men at Westminster would support them, even in war – let alone after. They would face execration whether they won or lost. They never faltered.

The revolt in south Wales had begun with the Parliament's redundant local forces mutinying against their orders to disband, and had swollen into a general rising when their discontented officers joined hands with the strongly royalist gentry of Pembrokeshire. Cromwell was promptly sent against them with three regiments of foot and two of horse. He arrived to find them already defeated on 8 May at St Fagan's, but they were still holding out in the castles of Pembroke, Tenby and Chepstow. The last two surrendered to him during May, but Pembroke was strong and desperately defended. What with endless difficulties in bringing up siege artillery, and the hostility and poverty of the countryside, Cromwell's men were pinned down, with little but bread and water for diet, until July.

Meanwhile the threat had spread to Ireland when Lord Inchiquin, who had been fighting the Irish Confederates with singular brutality, changed sides and declared for the King and the Scots. Soon after, the Scottish Parliament voted to raise a new army by 21 May, and somewhat hopefully fixed its strength at 30,000 foot and 6000 horse. To prepare for its coming, Sir Marmaduke Langdale seized Berwick on 28 April, and Carlisle was secured next day for its old royalist governor Sir Philip Musgrave. Both men had recently been in Edinburgh and were raising soldiers fast in the northern counties. But they had to reckon with Fairfax's able lieutenant in the north, John Lambert, who at twenty-eight was now a Major-General, and had been doing wonders in bringing back the discontented troops of the Northern Association to loyalty and discipline. Lambert was strong enough to contain Langdale until the Scots invaded, and before that happened Fairfax planned to come north himself with the main body of the army.

But Fairfax was kept busy by trouble nearer home. London and the home counties had been in a militant mood for some weeks. The City streets were ablaze with bonfires on 27 March, the King's accession day, and the revellers halted passing coaches and forced their passengers to drink his health. A fortnight later a great mob surged along Fleet Street against Whitehall crying 'Now for King Charles', and there followed a night of violence in the City which forced the Lord Mayor to take refuge in the Tower. Cavalry restored order next day, though not without bloodshed. On 4 May 2000 men of Essex marched to Westminster to petition for the recall of the King and the disbandment of the army. Surrey followed suit twelve days later, and there was a bloody clash with the guards when the petitioners tried to force their way into the House of Commons. Before such pressures as these, Parliament began to weaken in its resolve not to treat with the King under duress. In answer to a petition from the City fathers, the Commons agreed to resume negotiations if Charles would give certain pledges.

So far the disturbances about London had been more or less spontaneous, for the royalist gentry in the adjacent counties were wisely holding their hands until the Scots were ready to invade. But a sudden popular uprising in Kent forced them into action. It was touched off on 21 May when the county committee at Canterbury tried to suppress another petition like those of Essex and Surrey, and it spread so fast that within very few days half a dozen Kentish towns and strong-points were seized and held for the King. Six ships of the Navy, lying in the Downs, also declared for him, and with their help the royalists secured Sandown, Deal and Walmer Castles and laid siege to Dover. The Kentish gentry were deeply committed by now, and they planned a general rendezvous at Blackheath on 30 May, to gather their forces for an attack on

London. But it was Fairfax who concentrated his available regiments at Blackheath that morning, and for the next three days he drove the royalists steadily back upon Maidstone. There, with the old Earl of Norwich, Goring's father, as their commander, they made their stand; but 10,000 half-hearted countrymen were no match for Fairfax's veterans, and Norwich escaped that night with less than a third of his force.

Most of the rest deserted, but Norwich would not admit defeat. He ferried his last 500 faithful supporters across the Thames, seized Bow Bridge and spent three days at Stratford, recruiting London apprentices and watermen in considerable numbers. Fairfax sent Colonel Whalley after him with some cavalry, but before they could catch him Norwich was saved by the outbreak of revolt in Essex. It began in Chelmsford on 4 June with an angry crowd carrying off the entire county committee as prisoners, and when Sir Charles Lucas took charge of it and roused the trained bands it soon became formidable. Norwich brought in his small following to swell it, and so did many other distinguished royalist officers. But a fair part of the Essex trained bands remained loyal to Parliament, and with these before him and Whalley close behind, Lucas decided to make for Colchester to recruit his forces.

There Fairfax caught up with him on 12 June. His infantry came up next day, having marched fifty miles in as many hours. He had about 5000 men, and he threw them at once against Lucas's levies, rather fewer in number, who were drawn up across the London road to bar his way into Colchester. The royalists resisted long and fiercely before they were finally driven back within the walls, and though Fairfax persisted until after midnight, every attempt to carry the town by storm was beaten back. This very gallant fight by Lucas's ill-armed infantry was to pin down Fairfax and a considerable part of the New Model to a siege which lasted almost as long as the war.

And so by the middle of June the risings in Wales, Kent and Essex were safely contained, though at a heavy cost in regular troops. More troops were held down in the south-west, which remained restless even after an insurrection in Cornwall had been quelled in May. In Yorkshire, there was trouble for Lambert when Pontefract Castle was betrayed to the local royalists on 1 June, for they made such damaging raids from its walls that he had to divert much of his small strength to besieging them. June also saw further attempts at revolt in north Wales, Northamptonshire and Lincolnshire. The cavaliers had not shot their bolt yet. Officers with commissions from the Prince of Wales were still at large in many parts, waiting for their chance to get into action. Prince Charles himself travelled late in the month from St Germain to Holland to meet the royalist ships of the fleet, now nine in number, and sail with them for England.

All depended now on whether Hamilton could take the field in time to keep the royalists' efforts alive and profit by their tying down of the New Model. He had missed the best moment at the end of May, but an invasion in June could still have been very dangerous. Lambert alone could not have held it; Fairfax and Cromwell were occupied hundreds of miles away. But Hamilton was unable to move until the back of his English allies had been broken, and his unreadiness spelt the King's doom and his own. The reason for it lay in the harsh political realities of Covenanting Scotland.

Royalism dared not show its face there now; the only parties which counted were Argyle's and the Hamiltons'. Both were pledged to the Covenant, and both would have liked to see the King rescued and restored on decent terms. The difference was that Argyle and the strict Covenanters, with the whole power of the Kirk behind them, would do nothing for Charles while he himself refused the Covenant, and would have none but fellow-Covenanters as allies. The Hamiltons on the other hand had the support of most of the nobles and gentry, who did not relish the huge power which the Kirk now wielded in politics and society. They needed the King back to redress the balance in the interests of their own order. They paid lip service to the Covenant, but they preferred an uncovenanted King to no King at all. And since Charles was too uncompromisingly loyal to Anglicanism to win much Presbyterian support in England, they had to rely on the help of the English royalists, whom the Kirk branded as malignants. For Scotland it was an impossible alliance. Hamilton was unlucky to live in a time and a land whose politics posed a choice between stark irreconcilables, and his vain efforts to drive a path between them, for himself and his master, gave his whole career its character of vacillation and subterfuge. Neither a very clever nor a very high-principled politician, at least he was to redeem this, his last and most disastrous enterprise, by a courage and nobility in defeat which matched the King's own.

The Kirk party raised an outcry as soon as the terms of the Engagement were published in February, for they saw at once how little it promised for the Presbyterian cause. Hamilton could control the new Scottish Parliament which met in March, but he had to push through the measures for raising an army in the teeth of the Kirk's opposition. He was forced to reject the clergy's demands that the King should first pledge himself to settling Presbyterianism in all three kingdoms and that Scotland should ally with none but Covenanters, for he was already deeply committed to the Queen, the Prince of Wales and the English cavaliers. So recruitment proceeded to the accompaniment of the ministers' curses, which had much to do with the slow pace of the work and the poor quality of the men enlisted. They affected the choice of commanders too. Leven, who was too old for the work, was threatened and cajoled into resigning the generalship, and Hamilton somewhat reluctantly undertook it himself. His only venture in the Continental wars, long ago under Gustavus Adolphus, had been a near-fiasco, and from lack of trust in his own competence he was over-ready to defer to his subordinates. He badly needed a strong second-in-command. David Leslie was the obvious choice, but pressure from the Kirk made him and other good officers withdraw their services. The Kirk's opposition resulted in the post going to the Earl of Callander, who was not only on bad terms personally with Hamilton but as a near-royalist made the whole expedition doubly suspect. Callander had much experience commanding Scottish troops in the Dutch service, but it had made him a mere obstinate stickler for Dutch methods and discipline, and the authority he assumed in tactical matters far outran his talents. He was accused of building up his own faction in the army, and he habitually opposed Hamilton's views with a heat and arrogance to which the commander-in-chief too easily gave way. The Lieutenant-Generals of the Horse and Foot (respectively) were better men and better soldiers: John Middleton, who had served with Waller, and William Baillie, who had fought bravely at Marston Moor.

Delayed by all these dissensions and denunciations, a general levy was imposed throughout Lowland Scotland during May and June. It met tough resistance, especially in the fanatically Presbyterian west: Glasgow was only kept quiet by billeting troops on the angry burgesses, and in Ayrshire the clergy led an armed rising at Mauchline which had to be suppressed by military force. By the end of the month Hamilton's army was less than a third of its projected strength and in no shape for serious fighting. Yet Langdale, whom Lambert had penned in Carlisle, was sending constant appeals for relief, and all over England the royalist effort looked like collapsing unless it received strong support at once. Lanark advised postponing invasion till the army had dealt with the rising threat of rebellion at home, but Lauderdale was for marching into England at once, and his advice prevailed. So Hamilton crossed the border on 8 July with about 9000 men, two thirds of them infantry, and those so raw that most of them had still to learn how to handle pike and musket. That had not prevented them from behaving with such violence and lawlessness that their country was glad to see the back of them. The army was short of ammunition and without a single gun. To move its wagons it had to find horses and drivers in the country through which it marched, with the result that Hamilton often had to wait in the rear of the march until they could be brought in, and then convoy them with his own guard of horse.

To add to the troubles of this unlucky expedition, England had the worst summer in living memory. The weather was not just the familiar stuff that has taught philosophy to generations of Lakeland holidaymakers and Old Trafford patrons; the relentless rains, the cold, the storms and the bitter winds were unparalleled for the time of year, and much of continental Europe suffered them too. Parliament ordered a day of fasting and humiliation so that the nation might bewail its sins and implore God to send more seasonable weather, but the sins of the nation must have been a bad business, for the rains and tempests did not relent. They made tame rivers unfordable and turned country roads into quagmires; cavalry found the going a nightmare, musketeers could not keep their match alight, and more than one march was postponed for fear of the toll which sickness would take if the army slept in the open.

On entering England, Hamilton paused for six days at Carlisle. Musgrave handed the town over to him, and Langdale brought him the fine little force of about 3000 foot and a few hundred horse that he had raised in the northern counties. Lambert had fallen back on Penrith, for though he had recently been reinforced by some stout Lancashire levies under Colonel Ralph Ashton his strength was only a fraction of his opponents'. Hamilton was slow in going after him. His cavalry caught Lambert's outside Penrith on 14 July, but his hopes of a battle were dashed because his infantry became benighted on the road several miles back. Three days later he again attacked Lambert in Appleby, and again (though only after several hours' skirmishing) Lambert made a safe retreat. Hamilton then quartered for the rest of the month at Kirkby Thore, between Penrith and Appleby, waiting hopefully for the regiments which were still being raised when he left Scotland. Those that came in were far below strength, and brought his numbers (excluding Langdale's men) only to about 10,000 foot and 4000 horse. One other force, however, was on its way: 2100 horse and 1200 horse under Sir George Monro from the veteran Scottish army in Ulster. They were having a tough journey. Dogged by two of the Parliament's men-of-war, they had to cross the Irish Sea in small vessels by night, only to find themselves, as they marched through Galloway, railed at from the pulpits, shunned by the gentry and refused quarters by the countrymen.

Lambert was now posted about Bowes and Barnard Castle, with defences out on the high pass over Stainmore. He was anticipating a thrust by the Scots over the Pennines, while remaining prepared to threaten their flank should they advance through Lancashire. Help was at last on the way to him. Pembroke Castle finally surrendered on 11 July, and Cromwell lost no time in heading for Yorkshire. Sending much of his cavalry on in advance, he took with him only 3000 foot and 1200 horse. He had to make a wide detour through the midlands, for after so much hard service and foul weather his infantry were marching in tattered footwear or none at all, and he badly needed the 1500 pairs of shoes from Northampton and stockings from Coventry the Derby House Committee had ordered for him. These he collected at Leicester on 1 August, and two days later at Nottingham he picked up some contingents of local forces from Leicestershire, Nottinghamshire and Derbyshire which had been summoned to strengthen him. But these were not the only reasons for his marching so far east. He had to make sure of joining Lambert before meeting the Scots, for even together their forces would number less than half the enemy's, and like Lambert he probably expected Hamilton's next move would be into Yorkshire. What after all was likelier than that the Scots would try to relieve Pontefract? At any rate he was taking no chances, and he wrote to Lambert ordering him not to engage them till he himself came up.

Back in London, the news of Hamilton's entry into England arrived just after five days of alarm over a dangerous royalist insurrection which had broken out at Kingston, led by the turncoat Earl of Holland and the young Duke of Buckingham. It had been suppressed before it gathered much strength from the City, but a mob of apprentices and others showed their sympathy with it by trying to rescue the prisoners as they were brought back to London. The Commons declared, though only after a long debate, that the Scottish invaders were enemies to

the kingdom and that all who adhered to them were rebels and
traitors. But the Lords would not concur. Under constant pressure from petitions and demonstrations for the King, both
Houses were weakening, and the question was no longer
whether to negotiate with him but simply where and on what
terms. The Commons gave way to the Lords on 28 July and
agreed to treat without any prior pledges from Charles, though
they stipulated that the treaty should be on the Isle of Wight
and not in London. By that time further movements of insurrection had been quelled at Horsham, Hereford and Newark,
and plots to seize Portsmouth and Oxford had been foiled. But
the Governor of Scarborough Castle had declared for the King,
and the Prince of Wales now lay in the Downs with eleven
ships of the fleet, seizing merchant vessels and demanding ran-
som for them from the City of London. Deal and Sandwich
Castles, like Colchester, were still held by the royalists, and
there was a gleam of hope for them yet if Hamilton would
only move quickly.

But Hamilton seemed paralysed. His army was bringing
misery to the poor north country, suffering as it was a severe
dearth from the last bad harvest and facing ruin in the next
one. The soldiers' plundering and violence passed all bounds;
even the officers who fought with them admitted their incorri-
gible indiscipline. They stripped the dwellings where they
quartered down to the very pothooks, drove off great herds of
cattle and flocks of sheep, kidnapped children and ransomed
them to their parents at the sword's point. So many women
accompanied them out of Scotland, and so completely did they
take possession wherever they descended, that it came to be
believed that Hamilton had promised his followers the right
to settle in the land they won. Large numbers of Cumberland
and Westmorland folk had become refugees in neighbouring
counties. Resentment everywhere rose against the invaders,
'who', as *Mecurius Britannicus* put it, 'would gladly pester us
once more, and bring in their lice and Presbytery once more
amongst us'. 'Here', reported another newswriter from the

midlands, 'seems to be a great willingness to join against the Scots, rather than against any other party in England.'

The lull in the campaign brought no comfort to Lambert's men. 'We had miserable marches and most pitiful quarters in this barren and undone country', wrote one of them. Another gives a glimpse of Colonel Harrison and other senior officers breakfasting off bean bread, butter and water, adding 'therefore judge you what the poor soldiers have'. Much of their time indeed was spent in foraging, and often with scant success. The only action they fought between Appleby and Preston was on 26 July, when some Scots attacked their positions on Stainmore and forced them back to Barnard Castle. But they apparently returned to their defences on the pass, and Hamilton did not follow up his probe. Perhaps the feeblest part of his generalship was that during a whole month he made so little effort to bring Lambert to battle while he had him so heavily outnumbered. A victory might not only have brought in many of the northern royalist gentry who so wisely stayed at home; it might have enabled him to meet Cromwell, when he came, with overwhelming superiority in numbers.

Hamilton indeed seemed thoroughly undecided what to do. Only at the end of July did his council of war make a tentative decision to advance through Lancashire rather than Yorkshire, but when two days' march had brought him to Kendal on 2 August he halted again for another week. Guns, ammunition, transport horses, oatmeal – all were still deficient. Langdale, now based on Settle, showed signs of going off on his own to the relief of Pontefract, but when he failed to persuade the Governor of Skipton Castle to betray it to him he tried no further. Lambert acted sensibly to these moves by withdrawing to Richmond, then Ripon and finally (on 7 August) to Knaresborough. At about that time Monro arrived at Kendal ahead of his troops, but the much-needed stiffening they might have given to Hamilton's raw units was lost through a dispute over precedence. Monro would not take orders from Callander, and Callander would not tolerate Monro having an independent command; so these seasoned men from Ulster were posted

at Kirkby Lonsdale with two northern infantry regiments
(Musgrave's and Sir Thomas Tyldesley's), with orders to wait
for the guns which were still expected from Scotland. Hamilton then moved forward to Hornby on the 9th, and paused
there for another five days.

Cromwell meanwhile had reached Doncaster on the night
of the 8th, and waited there briefly for ammunition to reach
him from Hull. Two evenings later he attacked the royalists
in Pontefract and drove them back into the castle. Having
tightened up the siege, he took off with him the more experienced troops which had been engaged in it and left in their
place the midland forces which he had recently collected. His
forward regiments met Lambert's between Leeds and Knaresborough on the 12th, and the soldiers cheered the two commanders as they rode round their troops together. They still
had less than 9000 men between them, but as one of Lambert's
captains wrote they were 'a fine smart army, fit for action'.
At last they were going over to the attack.

Hamilton knew nothing of this. At Hornby another council
of war debated heatedly whether to continue through Lancashire or strike across the Pennines for the most direct route
to London. Middleton and Turner spoke for the Yorkshire
route, urging that it offered better cavalry country, whereas
the prevalent enclosures of Lancashire would only enable the
better training and fire-power of the enemy musketeers to tell
with greater effect. Callander seemed indifferent or undecided,
but Baillie was for Lancashire.[1] Hamilton in the end chose
Lancashire in the hope of bringing in more royalist forces that
way, especially some which were in arms under Lord Byron
in north Wales. He also seems to have set his heart on capturing Manchester. Much as he was later blamed for this decision, an advance by way of Skipton would only have delivered

1. Burnet in his *Memoirs of the Dukes of Hamilton* makes Hamilton and Baillie favour Yorkshire, and Callander and Langdale Lancashire. But his book is an apologia for Hamilton and blames Callander for every doubtful decision, so I follow the memoirs of Sir
James Turner, who was actually present.

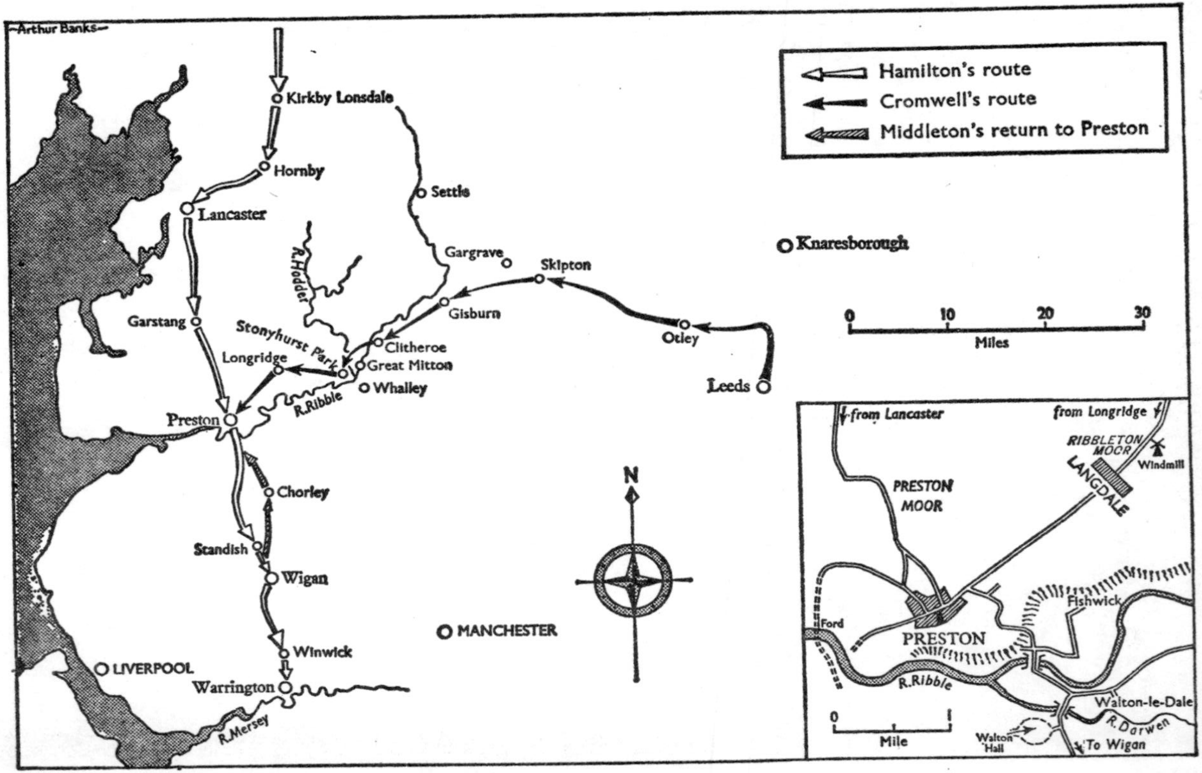

Arthur Banks
Hamilton's route
Cromwell's route
Middleton's return to Preston
Kirkby Lonsdale
Hornby
Lancaster
Settle
Gargrave
Skipton
Knaresborough
Gisburn
Garstang
R. Hodder
Stonyhurst Park
Clitheroe
Great Mitton
Whalley
Longridge
R. Ribble
Otley
Leeds
Preston
Chorley
Standish
Wigan
Winwick
Warrington
LIVERPOOL
MANCHESTER
R. Mersey
N
0
10
20
30
Miles
from Lancaster
from Longridge
RIBBLETON MOOR
Windmill
LANGDALE
PRESTON MOOR
Fishwick
Ford
PRESTON
R. Ribble
Walton-le-Dale
R. Darwen
Walton Hall
To Wigan
0
1
Mile

The Preston Campaign

him more certainly into Cromwell's hands; the time for a descent through Yorkshire had passed weeks ago.

On 14 August the Scots set out on their fatal march from Hornby to Preston, without a notion that Cromwell had quartered the night before at Otley and would make Skipton that very day. Langdale afterwards claimed that he rode over from Settle on the 13th to report the approach of enemy troops, but he did not identify them as Cromwell's. Had he done so, even Hamilton would not have strung out his forces as he now did. Hamilton in fact allowed himself to be persuaded by his cavalry commanders, who did not want to compete for scanty quarters and scantier provisions with the rest of the army, to let them march far in advance of it. The result was that when the foot (with only a small cavalry rearguard) approached Preston, Callander and Middleton with the bulk of the horse were sixteen miles farther south at Wigan. Hamilton probably thought his flank secure enough, with Langdale moving down Ribblesdale from Settle and detachments of Callander's horse out near Clitheroe. So it might have been, if these forces had sent him better intelligence. But he evidently heard nothing when Cromwell's son Henry, then a captain in Harrison's regiment, led out a cavalry patrol from Skipton and chased a party of Langdale's out of Gargrave. He knew equally little of Cromwell's advance to Gisburn on the 15th. Even next day, when Cromwell's forward patrols captured Colonel Tempest and a party of royalist horse at Waddow near Clitheroe, and at least one other royalist colonel had his quarters beaten up, no news reached Hamilton.

By that time Cromwell was marching where the knotted muscles of the high Pennines relax into the pastoral slopes and fertile closes of the lower Ribble. Three miles past Clitheroe, at the bridge over the Hodder, he held a vital council of war. The question was whether to cross the Ribble to Whalley by the last bridge above Preston and intercept the Scots' advance somewhere to the south, or keep the north bank of the river and attack them in Preston itself. A lucky piece of false intelligence, that Monro was on the march to join Hamilton and that Hamilton would probably wait for him, helped Cromwell to choose the second and bolder course, but other considerations moved him too. If he placed himself across the Scots' path south of the Ribble, he might have to be content with a partial engagement and leave them the option of retreating upon Monro or into Scotland. But an attack north of the river could give him the chance of interposing himself between them and their line of retreat and annihilating them utterly. That is what he proposed to do. That night, the last before the battle, his army rested in the park of Stonyhurst Hall. Langdale had his quarters only three miles away, and this time he did learn who his dangerous neighbour was and sent prompt word to Hamilton. But the alarm was scouted by 'an eminent personage' – probably Callander, who had ridden back from the cavalry quarters at Wigan – and no action was taken on it.

Cromwell on the other hand knew just where to find his adversary. He made as early a start as he could on the 17th, with the single thought of striking, and striking hard, before the far more numerous forces opposed to him could recover from their surprise and dispersal. He had 8600 men[1] to throw against about 14,000 of Hamilton's and the 3000 foot and 600 horse of Langdale's. Behind them – Cromwell did not know how far behind – were nearly 3000 more Scots under Monro and perhaps 1500 northerners under Musgrave and Tyldesley. In fact they were much too far back to help, and Hamilton's own command was fatally weakened by the sixteen-mile gap between his infantry and most of his horse. Only Langdale's men now shielded him from Cromwell's spear-thrust, and Langdale, having made an even earlier start than his pursuers, was pulling back hurriedly towards Preston. Even so his rearguard was caught by Cromwell's van near Longridge and had to fight its way back to where, just over two miles north-east of the town, his main body was preparing to make its desperate stand. Langdale himself had ridden straight on to report to

1. Cromwell's own estimate: composed of 4000 foot and 2500 horse and dragoons of the New Model, with 1600 and about 500 horse raised in Lancashire.

Hamilton and Callander. He found them on Preston Moor, a
mile and a quarter north of the town, with the Scottish infantry drawn up in preparation for marching south across the
river. Either they would not be convinced, or Langdale himself did not even know,[1] that Cromwell's whole army was
upon them, for Hamilton ordered the infantry to cross the
bridge. Langdale's troops, he concluded, should suffice to hold
off a mere harassing attack.

Half an hour later, Langdale was back with his men just in
time to see Cromwell's forlorn hope come upon them. His
position across the road into Preston was a strong one – as it
needed to be, outnumbered as he was and with very few
cavalry. The road itself was a deeply sunken lane, clogged with
mud and easily commanded by musket fire. On either side of
it lay enclosures intersected by frequent hedges and ditches,
which his musketeers lined; these and the waterlogged condition of the ground made normal cavalry tactics impossible.
Before this main position lay the more open expanse (mainly
north of the road) of Ribbleton Moor, where Langdale had
stationed outposts of both horse and foot.[2] These were engaged by the 200 horse of the forlorn under Major Smithson,
who drove them back and skirmished with them until his supporting infantry, 400 men under Major Pownall and Captain
Hodgson, came up. Before half of them had drawn up on the
edge of Ribbleton Moor, and while the main body of the
army was still four miles behind, Cromwell himself came on
the scene. Hodgson describes what ensued:

> The general comes to us, and commands us to march; we
> not having half of our men come up, desired a little patience.
> He gives out the word 'march!' And so we drew over a little
> common [Ribbleton Moor] and came to a ditch, and the

1. He knew of Cromwell's own proximity, but he had also been
misinformed that the parliamentarians had divided their forces and
sent part of them by way of Colne to defend Manchester.

2. The positions as described by Cromwell and Captain Hodgson
can be located with the help of a fine and almost contemporary MS.
map in the Lancashire County Record Office (press mark *DXX
194/28*).

enemy let fly at us, a company of Langdale's men that was newly raised. They shot at the skies, which did so encourage our men that they were willing to venture upon any attempt; and the major [Pownall] orders me to march to the next hedge, and I bid him order the men to follow me, and there drew out a small party; and we came up to the hedge end, and the enemy, many of them, threw down their arms, and run to their party, where was their stand of pikes, and a great body of colours.

The forlorn then held Langdale's main body engaged till the rest of the army had made its slow way forward through the narrow lane from Longridge. Smithson's horsemen, pushing up the lane, were momentarily driven into retreat by some Scottish lancers – almost the only reinforcement Hamilton sent Langdale during the fight. But the lancers were forced back in their turn, and in their flight Hodgson stepped into the lane, dismounted one of their officers and took his horse. By about four o'clock Cromwell had enough horse and foot on the spot to range them in a swiftly improvised order of battle and commit them to a full-scale attack. It was no set-piece battle as at Marston Moor or Naseby. There was little for the horse to do but try to hack its way through the lane, a task for which Harrison's regiment and Cromwell's own were detailed, with another in reserve. Two more cavalry regiments were ordered out to the right and the rest to the left, to explore any weaknesses in Langdale's flanks, if the ground allowed. But inevitably the infantry bore the brunt of the struggle, 'they often coming to push of pike and to close firing, and always making the enemy recoil', as Cromwell himself described it. Read's, Dean's and Pride's regiments fought on the right of the lane, and Bright's and Fairfax's on the left, with Ashton's Lancashiremen initially in reserve.[1] They forced Langdale's men back hedge by hedge, but they were made to fight hard. It was

1. Thus Hodgson; but *The Moderate Intelligencer* (17-24 Aug.) writes as if there was a first line consisting of Bright's, Fairfax's and the Lancashire regiments, and a second of Read's (*alias* Overton's), Dean's and Pride's. Very possibly this describes a later stage of the fight when it became concentrated south of the lane.

a small action in terms of numbers, but Hamilton's fate, and ultimately King Charles's, depended on it. Hodgson gives us another glimpse of it as, now mounted, he was sent off to report a dangerous situation to his colonel, who was himself 'deeply engaged both in front and flank':

> There was nothing but fire and smoke; and I met Major-General Lambert coming off on foot, who had been with his brother Bright; and coming to him, I told him where his danger lay, on his left wing chiefly. He ordered me to fetch up the Lancashire regiment; and God brought me off [safely], both horse and myself. The bullets flew freely; then was the heat of the battle that day. I came down to the moor, where I met with Major Jackson, that belonged to Ashton's regiment, and about three hundred men were come up; and I ordered him to march. But he said he would not, till his men were come up. A sergeant belonging to them asked me where they should march? I showed him the party he was to fight; and he like a true-bred Englishman marched, and I caused the soldiers to follow him; which presently fell upon the enemy, and losing that wing the whole army gave ground and fled.

Cromwell himself paid tribute to the courage of the Lancashiremen, whom Hodgson pronounced 'as good fighters and as great plunderers as ever went to a field'. But tribute is also due to Langdale's men, who against odds of far more than two to one maintained the fight for four hours,[1] and more than once recovered ground from their attackers, before they were finally overcome. They left many dead, and not a few were trampled into the mire of that horrible lane beneath the hooves of Cromwell's cavalry. In the later stages the fighting was mainly south of the lane, as they fell back in short bounds towards the Ribble bridge. But the Scots had failed to secure a lane which covered the bridge (probably the one from Fishwick) and they found their retreat cut off that way by Crom-

1. Cromwell's estimate: Langdale thought six hours. But after Cromwell launched the main body of his infantry, according to *The Moderate Intelligencer*, the crucial stage of the fight lasted about an hour.

well's cavalry of the left. They fell back into the town in disorder, pursued by Cromwell's and Harrison's cavalry regiments, and those who survived were soon all made prisoners.

It had been too late to save them when Hamilton, still on Preston Moor, at last became convinced that they were bearing the full weight of Cromwell's attack. He got Turner to dispatch a few hundred foot to them with some badly-needed barrels of powder; he also sent to Middleton to bring the cavalry back from Wigan and to Baillie to stop the infantry crossing the bridge. His immediate idea was to form up for battle on Preston Moor, though as yet the only cavalry he had with him was his troop of life guards; the rearguard regiments which had marched with the foot had not yet come up from their quarters. But when Callander found the infantry halted north of the bridge he rode off in a temper to remonstrate with his commander-in-chief. He argued that on Preston Moor, without adequate cavalry support against Cromwell's troopers, the Scottish infantry could be overrun in spite of its two-to-one advantage. The only safe course was to get them over to the same side of the river as Middleton's cavalry, who could be brought to rejoin them in time to make up an army fit to fight Cromwell next day. This might have made sound military sense, given staff-work less hopeless than Hamilton's, but it meant abandoning Langdale's men (who were still fighting) to their fate. Hamilton as usual gave way. Baillie led his infantry over the river, all but two brigades which were to hold the bridge.

Soon after Cromwell's leading troops broke into Preston town the bridge came under attack, and Hamilton's small party was in danger of being cut off from the rest of his army. Hamilton stayed on the Moor for his rearguard regiments of horse, which he ordered to make their way back to Monro. But the retreat soon became a headlong flight when Cromwell sent a body of horse chasing after them for ten miles through the rough and miry lanes towards Lancaster. Hamilton was not with them; at whatever risk he meant to rejoin his infantry. Callander had now crossed the bridge with them, and Hamilton had only Langdale, Turner, a few other gentlemen and his own troop with him. They first tried to cross the river by the ford a mile east of Preston, but the rains had made it a ford no longer. They were then strongly attacked by two troops of enemy horse on the outskirts of the town. Turner tried to rally some fleeing musketeers and get them to line the hedges to cover his general's retreat, but Hamilton, seeing how little fight was left in these men, himself led a charge against his assailants. Twice with conspicuous personal courage he beat them back, and twice they came at him again, but a third charge drove them far enough away to allow the party to swim the swollen river to the safety of the south bank. Thence it made its way to where Baillie had formed up the bulk of his infantry among easily defended enclosures near Walton Hall, on the gentle hill which rises a quarter of a mile south of the river Darwen.

The fight for the Ribble bridge was now raging. Fairfax's foot regiment and the Lancashire levies, supported by cavalry, pressed hard on the Scots brigades which held it. From his position south of the Darwen Callander sent forward 600 musketeers to reinforce the defenders, but as they crossed the flat expanse between the two rivers they were driven back by a hail of musket fire from the steep slope which rises between the Ribble and Preston. The slope was then chequered with small enclosures whose hedges and houses gave considerable advantage of ground and cover to the troops attacking the bridge. The Scots brigades defended it grimly for two hours, but they were finally forced from it by a fierce charge of pikes into the very mouths of their muskets. The smaller bridge over the Darwen was carried soon after, and all the Scots survivors driven back up the hill to the south and south-west of it.

Though night was beginning to fall now, a body of Cromwell's horse and foot still pressed up the slope after them and drove in their outposts upon their main body beyond Walton Hall. Here was a rich prize for a hard day's fighting: Hamilton's wagons, stranded now that the countrymen who had been pressed unwillingly into transporting them had taken the chance to slip off home with their horses. They were dragged off almost under the noses of the army which depended on them; one which overturned as it was brought triumphantly down the slope spilled all Hamilton's plate before the eyes of its captors.

Darkness brought a brief relief from the tensions of battle, but little comfort to either army. The weather was as foul as ever. A few lucky regiments, like Hodgson's, found good quarters in Preston, but most of Cromwell's troops lay down where they had finished fighting, south of the Ribble bridge, and his forward units remained beyond the Darwen almost within musket-shot of the Scots' outposts. He had already taken at least 4000 arms and almost as many prisoners, and he reckoned the enemy dead at a thousand. But that still left them still much stronger than him in numbers, and most of them had not even fought yet. His main concern was to prevent them escaping northwards, so he kept some companies of Ashton's Lancashiremen posted at Whalley to cover the next bridge over the Ribble at Great Mitton, and ordered seven troops of horse (which had also presumably missed the battle) to join them there from Clitheroe. He thought at this stage that the cavalry his men had pursued from Preston Moor towards Lancaster was the main body of Scottish horse, and he expected their foot to try to follow them or make their own way back to Monro.

But the Scots had other intentions. While the soldiers, weary, wet and hungry, improvised huts for shelter, Hamilton summoned his commanders for a hurried council of war. Callander spoke first and urged that they should march away by night to meet Middleton's cavalry on the road from Wigan. Only Baillie and Turner dissented, pointing out how much they risked by retreating in the face of such cavalry as Cromwell's, and by trying to move exhausted troops on such a black, wet night through sunken lanes deep in mud. Worse, it would mean abandoning all their ammunition. But the vote went against them, and the order was given for a drumless march. All the powder except what the soldiers carried was to be

blown up by a long fuse three hours after their departure, but
whether through rain or slackness it fell intact into Cromwell's
hands.

At least the Scots made their get-away unperceived. They
had a long start down the Wigan road before Cromwell knew
enough about it to send Colonel Thornhaugh after them with
two or three regiments of horse. But everything else went
wrong for them. They missed their own cavalry completely.
There were two routes from Preston to Wigan, and while the
unsupported infantry were stumbling and splashing their way
southward down the westerly one towards Standish, Middleton was advancing northward to their help by the other through
Chorley, where Langdale met him in the middle of the night.
Middleton, as he approached the Darwen, found not his own
army but the enemy's, and he got a hot reception; indeed it
was probably his appearance that awoke Cromwell into sending
Thornhaugh in pursuit. Middleton naturally turned and picked
up the tracks of the Scottish foot, but he was closely followed
and forced to skirmish all the way. Thornhaugh indeed pressed
one charge too rashly home and was killed, pierced by three
Scottish lances. But his troops did much execution, and the
main body of the army which followed them saw Scottish
corpses by the roadside all the way to Wigan.

Cromwell was pursuing now with no more than 3000 foot
and 2500 horse and dragoons. He had had few casualties, but
he had ordered the Lancashiremen back into Preston to guard
the prisoners and garrison the town against a possible attack
by Monro and the forces to the north, and some of his cavalry
were still dispersed after the pursuit from Preston Moor towards Lancaster. The Scottish horse still outnumbered his
own, and he probably did not exaggerate in estimating their
foot at 7000 or 8000 when they set out. But what with exhaus-
tion and demoralization, the darkness and confusion at the
start and the drenching all through the ensuing day, that march
to Wigan thinned them out considerably. Still quite early on
the morning of the 18th they turned and stood on some high
ground near Standish, and Middleton's cavalry, which had

been covering their rear, came up with them. But they did not stay to face Cromwell. The powder in the soldiers' flasks was soaked, and since they had left all their store of ammunition behind there was no more to be had. Middleton again covered their retreat into Wigan.

Even there they dared not rest. Hamilton's only hope now was to make for Warrington, where the Mersey would give him a stronger line to hold and he could perhaps make contact with Byron's forces. His utterly weary soldiers left Wigan that same evening for another night march, while Middleton skirmished with Cromwell's vanguard just north of the town. One at least of Middleton's regiments was put to rout; the alarm reached Sir James Turner as he was marching the last brigade of foot through the town. Turner formed up his pikemen shoulder to shoulder in the now moonlit market square and sent word to the brigades ahead of him to march on; then, when the beaten horsemen galloped up in disorder, he ordered the pikemen to open their ranks and let them through. They refused. Now in the last irrational stages of fatigue and failure, they scented treachery everywhere. 'All of you are Cromwell's men!' they shouted to Turner, and two of them ran at him with their pikes. Wounded slightly and fearing a general mutiny, he rode over and told the cavalry to charge the pikemen, but at this they jibbed. So he got someone to set up a cry behind them that the enemy was upon them. That was enough; the cavalry spurred forward, the pikemen threw down their weapons and fled into the houses, and some who did not shift in time were trampled beneath the horses' hooves. But Middleton was still at his post, and soon he rode back through Wigan with other troops in better order. The townspeople were glad to see the Scots go; poor as they were for the most part and strongly royalist, they had been plundered 'almost to their skins'.

Cromwell quartered his troops that night in a field close to the town, 'being very dirty and weary [he wrote], and having marched twelve miles of such ground as I never rode in all my life'. Early next morning he resumed the pursuit, and his horse

and dragoons, riding ahead, were soon taking their toll of the
fugitives once more. Even now the Scots stopped to plunder
the houses as they passed, sometimes while their own comrades were being killed in the road outside. It was probably
food they sought, for they were half-starved. But they were
well ahead of Cromwell's main body, and they still had time
and heart to make a last stand. They chose a natural defile in
the lane just north of Winwick, which, protected by a formidable bank, was quickly improved by defence works into a strong
position. There they stood at bay to Cromwell's vanguard and
forced it to retreat. They held their ground for several hours,
and even when his main body came up they met charge with
charge at push of pike. Once they even made the enemy give
ground, though it was quickly recovered. But some local men
guided Cromwell's officers to where his infantry could take the
Scots in the flank, and after heavy fighting they were driven
into a little green just short of Winwick church. As the
slaughter became more and more one-sided the Scottish foot
finally broke, many making for the church to become prisoners,
the rest effecting their escape to Warrington. Cromwell esti-
mated that they left a thousand dead and twice as many prisoners at Winwick.

In Warrington, Cromwell found the bridge strongly barri-
caded and covered by defence works. But there was to be no
more fighting. Hamilton and Callander with most of the horse
had already made off, leaving orders to Baillie to make what
conditions he could for the infantry. Baillie was distracted; he
begged the officers about him to put a bullet through his head
to spare him the shame of surrender. But his men just would
not fight any more. He had less than 2600 left; they had
been two nights without sleep, they were mud-soaked almost
to their waists, they had been subsisting on two pounds of
victuals issued a whole week ago and had scarcely eaten for
two days. Barely half of them had kept their arms, and for
these there was no ammunition. Baillie had to give way to his
officers and send to Cromwell with an offer of capitulation.
Cromwell would not accept his proffered terms as they stood,

but after a parley with Baillie himself on the bridge he promised the Scots quarter for life and civil usage upon surrender of themselves and all their arms. Guarding them was no great problem; they would not escape if they could, so scared were they now of the local countrymen, who were bringing in prisoners in droves when they did not kill them on the spot. 'Ten men will keep a thousand from running away', Cromwell wrote. Indeed he had to sign passes for his own men, to save them from being taken for Scots and maltreated.

All that was left of the Scottish army was the fleeing cavalry, apart from Monro's regiments and a few others in the far north of Lancashire. Langdale's force was annihilated. The shortcomings of Hamilton's entire enterprise, alike in conception and execution, stood brutally exposed. He had reckoned too little with the spirit and temper of the Scottish nation, whose deep distrust of his whole purpose was the real cause of the fatal delay and subsequent weakness of his expedition. As a commander he was responsible for the wasted weeks in July, the failure to formulate a plan of campaign until a month after crossing the border, the waste of Monro's troops, the breakdown of intelligence that allowed Cromwell to catch him with his horse and foot a day's march apart, the muddle that caused them to miss each other in the night after the Preston fight, and all through the campaign the atrocious indiscipline which made the Scots hated as enemies even when affection for the King's cause was naturally strong. Cromwell held the initiative from the first shock on Ribbleton Moor to the final surrender – indeed after Langdale's initial defeat Hamilton's tactics hardly aspired higher than to get out of the clutches of an army which was still only half his own size. Cromwell had disposed of his small forces with economy and daring, and his thrust and aggressiveness had been matched by the fighting spirit and endurance of his troops. He reckoned he had lost less than a hundred men killed, including only two officers of field rank. But he had many wounded, and after three days of almost continuous action all his men were worn out, the cavalry especially – 'so exceedingly battered as I never saw them in all my life', he described them, and 'so harassed and haggled in this business that we are not able to do more than walk an easy pace after them [the fugitive Scottish cavalry]'. Nevertheless he dispatched Lambert in pursuit with over 2000 horse and about 1400 foot, and sent urgent messages to the commanders in Stafford and Leicestershire and the forces before Pontefract to help round them up.

Hamilton and his cavalry at first rode towards Chester, hoping to join Byron in north Wales. But before long they changed their minds – fortunately, for Byron was in no position to help them – and turning due south they spent a miserable night in the open near Malpas in Shropshire. Middleton had joined them on the way, but Lord Traquair and several other high-ranking officers quietly made off and gave themselves up, which did not improve the soldiers' morale. That night they debated whether to aim for Pontefract or Herefordshire, where Sir Henry Lingen was reported to be in arms for the King. But Lingen had been routed on the same day as Langdale, and it seems to have been some rumour of his defeat that made them head for Yorkshire, making first a wide detour to the south to evade their pursuers. The next two days' marches took them through Market Drayton and Stone to Uttoxeter, harassed at intervals by attacks from the local trained bands. Middleton managed to beat these off until an unlucky fall from his horse, soon after leaving Stone, delivered him a prisoner to the Staffordshire forces. The soldiers, their ranks already thinned by desertion, were in a panicky and mutinous mood when amid high winds and heavy rain they reached Uttoxeter. Soon after leaving next morning they flatly refused to go any further, and to Uttoxeter Hamilton was forced to return. There he was bidden to surrender by a trumpeter from the Governor of Stafford. That night he and other senior officers had the humiliation of being held prisoners within sight of the enemy trumpeter by their own men, who suspected a conspiracy by their commanders to desert them. At some stage Callander managed to ride off with such men as he could persuade to follow him, and Langdale too escaped with a few remnants of his northern horse. Callander got away to London and thence to Holland, but Langdale was captured in an ale-house near Nottingham. Hamilton however stuck to his men to the last. He was treating with the Governor of Stafford when Lambert came up and took over, and on the 25th he and all his remaining men became Lambert's prisoners. It is said that he was offered a safe-conduct into Scotland if he would order the surrender of Berwick and Carlisle, and that he refused.

Monro and the other scattered forces in north Lancashire gave no trouble. Monro heard before Hamilton of Cromwell's arrival at Skipton on the 14th, and fearing an attack on himself he beat a hasty retreat towards Appleby. He returned to Kirkby Lonsdale two days later when he heard that Cromwell had taken the Preston road, and the next he knew was when the first fugitives from Preston Moor gave the alarm to his guards shortly before dawn on the 18th. About 1200 of these fleeing horsemen came in, and Monro urged them to stay with him; but they had had enough, and made straight for home. The remains of Langdale's horse – only a few had fled south with Langdale himself – made their way back to rejoin Musgrave's and Tyldesley's regiments of northern foot. Tyldesley, who was besieging Lancaster Castle, went straight to Monro and urged that they should all march together to Hamilton's assistance. With the fugitives from Preston added to Monro's and the northern regiments, together with some Scottish units left around Kendal, he reckoned they could muster over 7000 men. Monro refused; his orders, in case Hamilton were attacked, were to fall back northward and secure himself. So after waiting a day or two for further news he retreated by a circuitous route to Berwick, whence he was called home urgently to deal with fresh troubles in Scotland. Cromwell was already in pursuit, but much too far behind to interpose between him and the border. Lanark, Hamilton's vicegerent in Scotland, refused to let the remains of the English forces which had fought so bravely with the Scots take refuge over the border, lest they should give Argyle a pretext to call in Cromwell's troops. So Musgrave, Tyldesley and the rest gathered at

Carlisle for a hopeless resistance, which ended only in October with their surrender on honourable terms at Appleby Castle.

The first consequence of Cromwell's momentous victory was the rapid collapse of all royalist resistance. Colchester surrendered to Fairfax on 28 August. The extreme rigour with which he conducted the siege, the hard terms he exacted and his harshness towards the prisoners – Lucas and another commander were shot – shows how even the chivalrous Fairfax, so little an enemy to monarchy or a friend to fanatics, detested this war as a wanton shedding of blood. Deal Castle capitulated a few days before Colchester, Sandown shortly after. The Prince of Wales, who the day before Preston had accepted the Scots' terms and agreed to sail for Berwick and join their army, had to return to Holland. Byron escaped by way of Anglesey to the Isle of Man. One or two fortresses still held out in the north, but Pontefract Castle was alone in prolonging its stubborn, hopeless resistance into March of the following year.

In Scotland, reaction against Hamilton and his Engagers culminated in a minor civil war. Argyle recovered his ascendancy, and Lord Eglinton called out the fiercely Presbyterian west in a rising known as the Wiggamore Raid. With old Leven's help, these insurgents gained possession of Edinburgh, and the Committee of Estates which had been Hamilton's obedient tool retired to Stirling under Monro's protection. Then on 21 September Cromwell's army crossed the border into Scotland. Next day Cromwell and Argyle met, and the two strong men, as different in temperament as in their religious and political ideals, struck a wary accord. Cromwell obtained the surrender of Berwick and Carlisle, Argyle the support of English forces for the total overthrow of his enemies at home. Four days later the Committee of Estates threw in its hand. Lambert advanced on Edinburgh with a strong cavalry force, and Cromwell followed him there on 4 October. Cromwell obtained the removal from office of all who had supported the Engagement, and leaving Argyle firmly in power set out three days later for England.

In England the outcome of the army's triumph was even more dramatic. Parliament welcomed the news of Preston – the Lords actually anticipated the Commons in ordering a day of thanksgiving – but neither House intended for a moment to let the army which had gained the victory influence the use that was made of it. Armies, of course, should be the obedient servants of their governments, but this was no ordinary army, and this government showed no signs of breaking the impasse created by the King's refusal to accept the consequences of defeat. Cromwell's first dispatch after Preston, written from Warrington the day after Baillie's surrender, hinted at the army's hopes:

> Surely, Sir, this is nothing but the hand of God, and wherever anything in this world is exalted, or exalts itself, God will pull it down, for this is the day wherein He alone will be exalted. It is not fit for me to give advice, nor to say a word what use should be made of this, more than to pray you, and all that acknowledge God, that they would exalt Him, and not hate His people, who are the apple of His eye, and for whom even Kings shall be reproved; and that you will take courage to do the work of the Lord, in fulfilling the end of your magistracy, in seeking the peace and welfare of the people of this land, that all that will live quietly and peaceably may have countenance from you, and they that are implacable and will not leave troubling the land may speedily be destroyed out of the land.

But within a day of two of reading these words, Parliament formally repealed the Vote of No Addresses, and on 18 September its commissioners met the King at Newport on the Isle of Wight to begin a treaty. In the long weeks of haggling which ensued, Charles, practising the delays and evasions he had exploited so often, gradually made concessions which he would never have considered had he really contemplated being bound by them. They were, on his own admission, made merely in order to my escape, of which if I had not hope, I would not have done . . . for my only hope is that they now believe I dare deny them nothing, and so be less careful of their guards.

The army could not bear to see the fruits of victory rotting in the hands of politicians who seemed more intent on defeating the aspirations of their own defenders than they had been on beating the Scots. The Presbyterian majority at Westminster extended the term fixed for the treaty time and again, even though all attempts to reach agreement with Charles over religion had broken down. Pressure was mounting in the army, both in the north and the south, to put a stop to it. Fairfax was not behind this, for he was unhappy at any threat to the King's person or office, and Cromwell during November was dallying over the siege of Pontefract in a state of deep indecision. It was Ireton who directed the next move. To meet the misgivings of Fairfax and others, the Council of Officers made a last direct approach to the King. When inevitably it failed, the officers presented a fateful Remonstrance to the Commons on 20 November, demanding that the King be brought to trial for his life. Cromwell now approved the Remonstrance; the Commons merely shelved it. On the 30th the officers declared their intention of dissolving Parliament and constituting a provisional government from the Independent MPs who supported their demands. Next day they put a stop to Charles's plans for escape by removing him to Hurst Castle, and the day after they marched their regiments into London.

Here followed a brief hitch in their plans. The Independents refused to countenance a dissolution by the army, and requested it to 'purge' the Commons instead. The officers had to choose between complying or setting up a naked military dictatorship. They complied. The Presbyterians gave them a pretext by voting that the King's thoroughly unsatisfactory answers to their propositions constituted 'a ground for the course to proceed upon for the settlement of the peace of the kingdom'. The army's answer next day was Pride's Purge – Colonel Pride's forcible exclusion from the Commons of the Presbyterians who insisted on reinstating the King. That same evening Cromwell arrived in London at last, his mind now fully made up. The rest of the tragedy now followed its famous course. The Independent Rump of the Commons erected a revolutionary tribunal called a High Court of Justice, and King Charles's head rolled on the scaffold at Whitehall on 30 January. Monarchy and the House of Lords were abolished, and England became a Commonwealth under the supreme authority of a fraction of a House of Commons elected more than eight years ago, and sitting now under the shadow of the army.

The King's life was not the last sacrifice demanded by the new order. In February a new High Court of Justice was constituted to try the leaders of rebellion and invasion in the late war. Of five men sentenced to death, three, including Hamilton, actually suffered public execution before Westminster Hall. Much as one could wish they had been spared, to Cromwell their crime was clear. It was

a more prodigious treason than any that had been perfected before; because the former quarrel was that Englishmen might rule over one another, this to vassalize us to a foreign nation; and their fault who have appeared in this summer's business is certainly double to theirs who were in the first, because it is the repetition of the same offence, against all the witnesses that God has borne, by making and abetting a second war.

Epilogue

Marston Moor Revisited

IT IS New Year's Day of 1660, and the scene is Marston Moor again. More than fifteen years have healed the scars of battle on that famous field, yet a body of cavalry is drawn up on it once more, and at its head rides Fairfax. Once again, his objective is to capture York. But York is now held in the name of the Commonwealth, and Fairfax's intention, though he does not declare it, is to help King Charles II recover his throne.

The English Revolution has taken many strange turns since the execution of Charles I, and Fairfax has been out of sympathy with most of them. He had no part in the trial of the King, and since 1650, when he resigned the generalship of the army, he has lived most of the time in a gouty retirement. His daughter has married the Duke of Buckingham, whom we met at the head of a royalist insurrection just before Preston, but he has resisted all attempts by the royalists to enlist his own active support. He has watched passively while the Rump of the Long Parliament, which ruled the Commonwealth for over four years, quarrelled with the army to which it owed its power, until Cromwell was goaded into clearing it from the House with a file of musketeers. He has seen the brief experiment of Barebone's Parliament give way to the Protectorate of Oliver Cromwell, with whose government he has had one or two angry brushes. He has made a rare appearance in public to attend the Parliament summoned by Richard Cromwell nearly a year ago, after Oliver's death. But it is the anarchy which has developed since Richard's fall from power last April that has spurred him into more decisive action.

Cromwell had spent his last years in trying, without sacrificing his essential ideals of religious liberty and 'a reformation of manners', to reconcile the moderate gentry, bridle the army and establish a reasonable constitution of checks and balances. Unfortunately his death left the army under miserably inferior leadership, and its more fanatical elements took their revenge on his son Richard. They were easily persuaded by scheming republican politicians and fire-eating sectarian preachers into believing that 'the good old cause' had been betrayed by the ambition of the house of Cromwell, and having overthrown Richard by a *coup d'état*, they were induced in a mood of witless enthusiasm to restore the Rump, just as it had sat six years ago. But within four months army and Rump were quarrelling again as they had done before, and in October 1659 Major-General Lambert carried out a second *coup* which closed the Parliament once more. From then until Christmas the only government the country had was a semi-military junto, led by the generals Lambert, Fleetwood and Desborough, which called itself a Committee of Safety. It was so generally hated that it failed to fulfil the most elementary functions of government, and England began to lapse into an anarchy such as even civil war had hardly brought in its train. Indeed the demonstrations and disturbances in many parts actually threatened the renewal of civil war. In London the tide of riots mounted, troops clashed almost daily with the citizens, the courts of law at Westminster ceased to sit, wealthy traders hurried their wares out of town and shut up their shops, and the City's commerce thinned to a trickle. Royalism began to mean more than drunken toasts and tavern-talk; the very small band that had never ceased to fight underground for Charles Stuart pricked up its ears. For monarchy now offered the sole hope of stable and legal government, and popular enthusiasm for the King's return was rising by leaps and bounds. But it was not yet safe to campaign for him openly. Those who wanted to see him home again clamoured either for a new, free Parliament or for the readmission of the 'secluded members' to the old one. A tolerably free general election would certainly have done the trick, but was almost too much to hope for yet. To recall the old Parliament, however, with the 'secluded members' reinstated – the Presbyterians, that is, who had been expelled by Pride's Purge after Preston – would be the next best thing.

These members had lost their seats for refusing to depose Charles I, so what more natural than that they should work towards restoring his son?

But the man to whom Charles II most owed his restoration did not support either of these demands. General George Monck was not going to let anyone call him a royalist. It is very unlikely that he was one yet. He simply demanded that the Rump should be restored to its authority, and he prepared to march to its help with the small but well-knit English army which he commanded in Scotland. He had no love for the Rump and no illusions about its political bankruptcy, but its tattered shreds of constitutional right gave him a pretext to intervene and put a stop to the suicidal folly of his fellow-officers in London. To stop him, the Committee of Safety had to send the bulk of its own troops northward under Lambert, and during the last weeks of 1659 the two armies faced each other across the Tweed. Lambert's, nearly 12,000 strong, was much the larger, but as the weeks went by its willingness to fight in a failing cause became, like its pay, increasingly uncertain.

This was where Fairfax could help immeasurably. If he could raise the Yorkshire gentry and rally those forces of Lambert's which had no heart for the Committee of Safety's quarrel, Monck might be spared the need to fight his way into England – and fighting was the last thing Monck wanted, for political no less than military reasons. Fairfax's was still a name to conjure with. To the Independents and the soldiers he still bore unstained the reputation of the New Model's victories, while the Presbyterians, since his opposition to the King's execution, and his subsequent withdrawal from public life, regarded him as one of themselves. But Fairfax fought shy at first of helping Monck. Much as he detested the army's recent usurpation, he did not want to pledge himself too far to the Rump, as Monck had done. But Monck sent his brother-in-law Thomas Clarges to reassure Fairfax that there was more to his intentions than he dared declare publicly, and that brought him round. After that the main problem was how to concert plans, for Lambert's whole army was soon posted between Yorkshire and Coldstream, where Monck had his headquarters. Fairfax's young cousin Brian, home for Christmas from Cambridge, solved it by undertaking a six days' ride by a wild route over the snow-covered hills and frozen rivers of Cumberland and Teviotdale, which after many hazards brought him into Monck's camp towards midnight on Christmas Day.

By then the Committee of Safety had just collapsed. Threatened and execrated on all sides, defied now by the fleet and the army in Ireland as well as by Monck, increasingly deserted by its own soldiers, it could struggle no longer, and on 26 December the Rump returned in triumph to Westminster. Neither Monck nor Fairfax changed their plans when they heard the news a few days later, for neither really hoped for much from the Rump.

On 30 December about 300 of the East Riding gentry and their retainers made their rendezvous near Malton, while Fairfax, so crippled with gout that day and in such pain from the stone that he had to ride in his coach, journeyed with a dozen friends to Arthington in lower Wharfedale to collect his West Riding friends. He did not expect large numbers, for the need for secrecy had limited his contacts, and he would have no royalists in his company. To have admitted them would have defeated his first object, which was to divide and disable Lambert's forces. Even his son-in-law Buckingham had to be sent home. The policy paid; before the first night was through, several cavalry troops had come over to him from Lambert, and he had word that a whole brigade, which had been brought back from Ireland last summer, was ready at Wetherby to obey his commands. On the 31st the East and West Riding parties joined forces at Knaresborough, while Lambert's regiments, alerted to their danger and demoralized by the news from London, were falling back confusedly into Yorkshire.

So it was that Marston Moor, close to both Wetherby and York, was chosen for the final rendezvous for Fairfax's Yorkshire friends and the Irish Brigade on New Year's morning.

The meeting did not go off quite smoothly. The officers who had deserted Lambert, including those from Ireland, wanted some assurance that Fairfax was acting in the interest of the Rump and not of the secluded members, so they caused a declaration of loyalty to the present Parliament to be read at the head of their troops and offered it to all present to subscribe. This was not to Fairfax's liking, but somehow he avoided signing. At any rate the 1800 men who had gathered on the Moor acclaimed him with loud shouts, and he led them off against York.

At about noon he drew them up before Micklegate Bar and sent a trumpeter forward to summon the city. Colonel Robert Lilburne, the Leveller leader's brother, whom Lambert had entrusted with its defence, was not only outnumbered; he was up against the defiance of the city fathers, the general hostility of the citizens and the inclination of his own men to throw in their lot with the forces outside. After parleying for as long as he could, he at length agreed to spare the city an assault, provided those who entered it engaged to adhere to the Parliament as now constituted (i.e. without the secluded members) 'against a King or any other single person whatsoever'. This stipulation not only cleared his conscience, it neatly divided his opponents. Such an engagement, which was just what the Irish Brigade wanted, so disgusted Fairfax that he tore it up, and disagreement reached such a pitch that the troops from Ireland drew up facing Fairfax's levies in the field towards Poppleton as if they would fight each other. But around four o'clock Fairfax agreed to let the forces which had deserted Lambert occupy York, while he quartered his own men in the fields outside.

That same day Monck's vanguard crossed the Tweed. When Monck himself followed the day after, all opposition had collapsed. Lambert had only a handful of officers and about fifty troopers still with him; the rest of his men were glad enough to obey the Rump's command to disperse to their former quarters. Lilburne had to submit unconditionally, and Fairfax entered York. The rest of the story has been told many times.

Monck's peaceful progress through a snowbound England became almost a triumphal march, even though he maintained his show of obedience to the Rump to the last. But on his arrival in London, the Rump sought to reduce his alarming popularity by sending him and his army to subdue the defiant City, which was threatening to refuse all taxes until a fully representative Parliament was assembled. Monck at first obeyed; and at this juncture the gentry of Yorkshire, headed by Fairfax and following several other counties' example, framed a declaration that until a new, free Parliament was called they too were not obliged to pay taxes. But before this document reached London Monck had turned on his crazy masters. On 11 February he sent the Rump a virtual ultimatum, giving it six days to issue writs for elections to all the vacant seats in the House. That night bells rang in every City steeple and bonfires blazed in every street, while round them the citizens symbolically 'roasted the Rump' by grilling steaks on long sticks. Ten days later, having received no satisfaction, Monck had the secluded members quietly readmitted to their places. The Rumpers, outnumbered now by their old Presbyterian opponents, were powerless; the Restoration was inevitable now. London had another night of bonfires and bell-ringing, and this time the King's health was drunk openly in the streets.

In March the Long Parliament provided for the summoning of its successor, then quietly dissolved itself at last. The general elections which followed reflected the great upsurge of national feeling for the old monarchy, and the temper of the new Parliament ensured that the Restoration would be unconditional. Many who had fought against Charles I shared in the rejoicing over his son's return, for many had contributed to it. Fairfax headed the commission which Parliament sent to greet the King at the Hague, and it was a horse from his stables that Charles later rode at his coronation. After that, a life of retirement was all Fairfax wanted; he probably did not envy Monck the shower of honours and rewards that fell on him. There were honours too for the Earl of Manchester, who became Lord

Chamberlain and a privy councillor. His old fellow-general and rival Sir William Waller looked in vain for reward, however, though he had been gaoled in the Tower for plotting a royalist rising in 1659.

For others who had fought with Fairfax and Cromwell the Restoration could only bring a heavy reckoning, especially if they had sat in judgement on Charles I. Major-General Harrison and Colonel Okey were among the thirteen regicides who were hanged, drawn and quartered. The body of Ireton, who had died on campaign in Ireland nine years ago, was exhumed with Cromwell's from Westminster Abbey, and both were hanged in their shrouds at Tyburn. Lambert and Vane, who were not regicides, were nevertheless tried for their lives and condemned to death, though only after the King had granted a petition from both Houses to spare their lives. Lambert languished in prison until his death in 1683, but Vane defended his principles at his trial, and Charles despite his promise intervened personally to have the death sentence carried out.

Among the royalist commanders, Rupert returned to England in honour and soon resumed the career as an admiral which he had begun in the second Civil War. The Marquis of Newcastle accompanied Charles on his journey home, and presented him with perhaps the most marvellously reactionary manual of advice ever tendered to an English sovereign.[1] But he soon retired to Welbeck, where honoured with a dukedom he devoted the last twenty-six years of his long life to his two passions, horses and literature. Hopton and Byron both died in exile, and Goring in the service of Spain. Langdale had escaped after his capture in the flight from Preston and fought for a while with the Venetians against the Turks. Now a baron, he was too poor to attend Charles II's coronation, and he died soon after it.

To follow the fortunes of the contestants further, to trace the progeny of their ideas and ideals, and to assess the long-term impact of the Civil War on church, state and society, would require another book, and a longer one. Perhaps one rather

1. See D. Ogg, *England in the Reign of Charles II*, I, 142-7.

obvious remark may be offered in conclusion. The Great Civil War was the last in English history, and amongst the deepest imprints it left upon the national consciousness were an abhorrence of militarism and a belief in surmounting crises by any means but violence. Because Englishmen had learned their lesson, the revolution which cost James II his throne was as bloodless as the Restoration which had brought his brother back to it. Once, in between, amid the frenzy of the Popish Plot, the spectre of civil war rose again. More perhaps than anything else, the cry of ''41 is come again' brought the nation back to its senses.

Bibliographical Note

(These notes are selective rather than exhaustive, but it is hoped that they will be more useful than a mere list of works and documents to the non-specialist reader who may wish to pursue the Civil War further, whether in other modern books or in the more important sources.)

GENERAL. Beside the classic account in S. R. Gardiner's *History of the Great Civil War* now stands Miss C. V. Wedgwood's *The King's War*, a fine and deeply sympathetic narrative, particularly strong on Scottish affairs. The late Colonel A. H. Burne and Brigadier Peter Young, in *The Great Civil War*, eschew all politics but offer useful professional comment on the battles. C. H. Firth's *Cromwell's Army* is only one of many works with which this great historian has illumined the war. C. H. Firth's and Godfrey Davies's *Regimental History of Cromwell's Army* is invaluable for tracing the careers of particular officers and units. B. H. G. Wormald's *Clarendon* and J. H. Hexter's *The Reign of King Pym* are important for the political background to the war. Clarendon's own *History of the Rebellion*, though unreliable on military matters, provides a wonderful gallery of portraits. Other old compilations of intermittent value are J. Rushworth's *Historical Collections*, John Vicars' *Parliamentary Chronicle* and Bulstrode Whitelocke's *Memorials of the English Affairs*. The *Calendar of State Papers, Domestic Series* is indispensable to serious study, and the Thomason Collection in the British Museum contains almost all the pamphlets and news-sheets published in the period; its published catalogue, though defective, is nevertheless a gold-mine. W. C. Abbott's *Bibliography of Oliver Cromwell* and *Writings and Speeches of Oliver Cromwell* are essential source-books.

BIOGRAPHIES. *The Dictionary of National Biography* is invaluable for all the major figures, especially where the work is Firth's. On the royalists, E. B. G. Warburton's old and unreliable *Memoirs of Prince Rupert and the Cavaliers* contains many valuable documents; Brigadier Young is preparing a modern study of the Prince. For an adequate life of Charles I we must await the forthcoming work of J. P. Kenyon. Newcastle's Duchess wrote a fulsome biography of her husband, but modern readers may prefer A. S. Turberville's account in *A History of Welbeck Abbey and its Owners* (Vol. 1). Of Cromwell, C. H. Firth's life remains after sixty years the best, though Maurice Ashley's *The Greatness of Oliver Cromwell* and John Buchan's *Oliver Cromwell* can also be recommended. M. A. Gibb's *The Lord General* is a pleasant life of Fairfax, but C. R. Markham's older biography is fuller on military matters. There is an admirable biography of Leven by C. S. Terry, a scholarly one of Okey by H. G. Tibbutt, an adequate one of Ireton by R. W. Ramsey and a mediocre one of Lambert by W. H. Dawson. Maurice Ashley's *Cromwell's Generals,* though good, is mainly concerned with the sixteen-fifties.

TURNHAM GREEN. Mainly based on Rushworth, Clarendon, Whitelocke, Vicars, the memoirs of John Gwynne, Sir Richard Bulstrode and Sir Philip Warwick, the diaries of John Rous (Camden Soc., 1856), D'Ewes (*B.M. Harleian. MSS. 164*) and Whitacre (*B.M. Add. MSS. 31,116*), the *Coke MSS.* (Historical MSS. Commission), the *Calendar of State Papers, Venetian Series, 1642-3,* and the following Thomason pamphlets (B.M. press marks): *E126.26, 44, 48; E127.8, 10, 12, 20; E242.10, 14.*

MARSTON MOOR. Pride of place goes to C. H. Firth's exhaustive account in *Transactions of the Royal Historical Society,* New Series, XII, where the sources are fully evaluated, and Ogden's and Stockdale's narratives printed. After that the best is by C. S. Terry in *The Life and Campaigns of Alexander Leslie*; he prints Simeon Ash's *A Continuation of*

True Intelligence, one of the best contemporary accounts, and *A Full Relation of the Late Victory,* a Scottish compilation which must be used with caution. Leonard Watson's *A More Exact Relation* (Thomason *E2.14*) is the best of the pamphlets; 'W.H.', *A Relation of the good successe of the Parliaments forces (E54.11)* has some independent value, and there are minor points in *E54.9, E54.20* and *E2.21. Historical Fragments Relative to Scottish Affairs* (Edinburgh, 1833) prints 'The Glorious and Miraculous Battel at York' and Robert Douglas's diary, both important. Fairfax's own *Short Memorials* are valuable as far as they go, but the *Memoirs of Denzil, Lord Holles* are more malicious than trustworthy. On the royalist side, Sir Hugh Cholmley's account is printed in *English Historical Review, V* (with the tract *Vindiciae Veritatis* in defence of Cromwell), and the journal of Prince Rupert's marches in *ibid., XIII.* Sir Henry Slingsby's *Diary* (ed. D. Parsons, 1836) deals with the battle briefly but vividly, and Thomas Fuller's *History of the Worthies of England* adds some interesting details. So do the document printed in Clarendon, *History of the Rebellion* (ed. W. D. Macray, 1888), III, p. 376n., and Arthur Trevor's letter in T. Carte's edition of the Ormonde papers (1739), I, 55-8.

For the subsequent political conflict, see J. Bruce and D. Masson (eds.), *The Quarrel between the Earl of Manchester and Oliver Cromwell* (Camden Soc., 1875); *Camden Miscellany, VIII*; Rushworth, V; *Cal. S. P. Domestic, 1644–5*; *Letters and Journals of Robert Baillie* (Bannatyne Club, Edinburgh, 1841), II.

NASEBY. There are no noteworthy modern accounts of the battle outside the standard works listed above, but R. N. Dore's 'Sir William Brereton's Seige of Chester and the Campaign of Naseby', in *'Transactions of the Lancs and Cheshire Antiquarian Soc., LXVII,* is a valuable piece of recent research. The royal army's movements can be followed in the journal of Rupert's marches (above) and in Richard Symonds' *Diary* (Camden Soc., 1859). Letters to and from the King's camp are printed in Hist. MSS. Comm., *1st Report* (*Lords MSS.*) and *Portland MSS., I*, and in the Bohn edition of Evelyn's *Diary, IV* (1887). Sir Samuel Luke's letter-books (*B. M. Egerton MSS. 786*), which throw much light on the New Model's movements, and from which extracts appear in Sir Henry Ellis's *Original Letters, 3rd series, IV*, are being edited for publication in calendar form by Mr H. G. Tibbutt.

The fullest contemporary account of the battle from the parliamentarian side is in J. Sprigge's *Anglia Rediviva* (1647), and from the royalist in Sir Edward Walker's *Historical Discourses* (1705) and in Slingsby's diary. Other important narratives are by Col. Wogan in Carte's Ormonde papers, I; by George Bishop and Col. Okey in *A more particular and exact Relation* (*Thomason E288.38*); by Rushworth (allegedly) in *An Ordinance of the Lords and Commons* (*E288.26*); also in *A more exact and perfect Relation* (*E288.28*), *A True Relation of a Victory* (*E288.22*; clearly less authentic), and 'W.G.', *A Just Apology for an Abused Army* (*E372.22*). Other Thomason tracts which yield minor points are *E288.3, 4, 5, 7, 8, 11, 27, 30, 31, 33, 35, 37, 45* (on the prisoners; cf. Hist. MSS. Comm. *7th Report, Verney MSS.*); *E262.7, 8, 10*. Whitelocke's *Memorials* provide some recollections of the battle by Col. D'Oyley of Fairfax's life guard.

PRESTON. Gardiner is good on Preston, and nothing considerable has been published on it since. The background to Hamilton's expedition is much illuminated by G. Burnet, *Memoirs of the Lives and Actions of James and William, Dukes of Hamilton*, Baillie's *Letters and Journals, The Memoirs of Henry Guthry* (1747) *and The Hamilton Papers*, ed. S. R. Gardiner (Camden Soc., 1880). Burnet also has a full account of the Preston campaign, based on material collected from participants, but being a heavily-weighted apologia for the Hamiltons it must be taken with caution. Cromwell's full dispatches are in W. C. Abbott (above), I; Langdale's narrative and other documents in *Civil War Tracts of Lancashire* (Chetham Soc., 1844); Musgrave's and Thomas Reade's narratives in *Scottish History Society Miscellany, II* (1904). Sir James Turner's excellent *Memoirs* (Bannatyne Club, 1829) and *A Letter from Holland* (*Thomason E467.21*) provide the two best narratives from the Scottish–royalist side. Captain Hodgson's vivid *Autobiography* (1806 and 1882) is supplemented by Capt. Samuel Birch's diary (Hist. MSS. Comm., *Portland MSS., III*) and E. Robinson's *Discourse of the Civil War in Lancashire* (Chetham Soc., 1864). Rushworth is useful. Of pamphlets, other than those already mentioned, only *The Moderate Intelligencer* for 17-24 August 1648 (*E460.35*) throws much light on the battle itself, but other Thomason tracts found useful for the campaign include *E453.5, 8, 10, 20, 21, 29, 34; E454.2, 3, 10, 14, 16, 19; E456.1, 5, 8, 9, 13, 17, 23; E457.16, 21, 28, 33; E458.17, 21; E459.1, 2, 19, 24; E460.12, 17; E461.9.*

The sources for the Epilogue are given fully in my article on 'Yorkshire and the Restoration' in *Yorkshire Archaeological Journal* (1958).

Index